Only Retire Once

HOW TO AVOID

The 9 Deadly Mistakes

OF RETIREMENT

Only Retire Once

HOW TO AVOID
The 9 Deadly Mistakes
OF RETIREMENT

ROY WILLIAMS, ChFC®

ONE OF *BARRON'S* TOP 1,200 ADVISORS

Only Retire Once
© 2014 by Roy Williams

Williams Family Press
31 Ocean Reef Dr., Suite C-208
Key Largo, FL 33037

Email: williamsfamilypress@gmail.com
www.onlyretireonce.com

ISBN# 978-0-9960521-0-8

Manufactured in the United States of America

Book cover design by George Foster
Interior design by Deborah Perdue of Illumination Graphics
Editing by April Michelle Davis of Editorial Inspirations and Anita Gabor Bartal

Source: Barron's "Top 1,200 Advisors," February 24, 2014, as identified by Barron's magazine, using quantitative and qualitative criteria and selected from a pool of over 4,000 nominations. Advisors in the Top 1,200 Financial Advisors have a minimum of seven years of financial services experience. Qualitative factors include, but are not limited to, compliance record and philanthropic work. Investment performance is not a criterion. The rating may not be representative of any one client's experience and is not indicative of the financial advisor's future performance. Neither Morgan Stanley Smith Barney LLC nor its Financial Advisors or Private Wealth Advisors pays a fee to Barron's in exchange for the rating. Barron's is a registered trademark of Dow Jones & Company, L.P. All rights reserved.

Disclaimer: The information in this book does not constitute legal advice. Please see a qualified and experienced estate planning attorney for advice on your specific situation.

DEDICATION

First, to the love of my life, Janet, and my three wonderful children, Roy III, Michael and Camryn, thank you for all your love and support during this book project and for your support throughout my career. Janet, you are the best wife, partner, spouse, mother and friend any man could ever ask for. And to my deceased parents, Jane and Roy Williams, for providing the foundation of who I am today and to my stepmother, Fawn Williams, for providing wisdom, love and support.

TABLE OF CONTENTS

Don't Underestimate How Long You Will Live
Deadly Mistake One – Outliving Your Savings
>Here's How to:
>• Making the Retirement Decision
>• Mapping Out a Lifestyle You Can Afford
>• Assessing Retirement Expenses and Income
>• Planning Your Working-Life Exit

Be Realistic About Retirement Expenses
Deadly Mistake Two – Failing to Plan the Life You Want
>Here's How to:
>• The Wisdom of No Debt
>• Job Loss and Other Unanticipated Financial Surprises
>• Healthcare Disasters
>• Home Location

Create a Realistic Budget and Stick to It
Deadly Mistake Three – Unrealistic Spending Expectations
>Here's How to:
>• Learn How Inflation Affects Budgeting
>• Determine the True Cost of Living
>• Budget for the Unexpected
>• Celebrate Being a Smart Consumer
>• Build a Budget on a Solid Foundation

I recently had lunch with a friend who happened to be passing through town on his way to a business meeting in New York. After catching up about our respective families and careers, he mentioned that he was thinking about retiring—or as he more accurately put it "thinking about what I want to do next."

My friend's attitude about what he expects from retirement reflects the outlook of a majority of my clients. For this generation, and the baby boom generation in particular, the word *retirement* just doesn't seem to fit. A more appropriate term might be *explorer, experience seeker, traveler*, or *continuous learner*. Clearly, my friend would be comfortable with any of these labels.

If any of these alternative labels would fit your post-retirement expectations, then this book is definitely for you. It will help you build a realistic plan to become the explorer, traveler, and experience seeker you might imagine as the life you'll lead after retirement. Still, there's nothing magical about the advice I give in this book to achieve this dream beyond a pragmatic and realistic approach to one important element of the plan—what it will ACTUALLY cost to fund your retirement adventures.

Before my friend left that day, he asked me what I thought was the biggest mistake people make in retirement planning. He was surprised that I had an immediate answer.

"That's easy," I said, "under-estimating the amount you think you'll spend."

While that might seem an obvious conclusion, most of the clients I advise are shocked by how much it *really* costs to fund their retirement vision. I don't expose my clients to the full, unvarnished scope of retirement costs for shock value, but rather to help my clients build a realistic retirement plan that ultimately will allow them to achieve more of the goals they set.

People are often surprised when I tell them I once wanted to be a social worker. But in my mind the two fields are not that far apart and are related in an important way—both are designed to help people achieve their life goals. That's how I see my job as a financial planner. After all, we have no more important responsibility than managing as best we can the money we earn so that it supports our family's needs today while funding the future life we envision for ourselves and those we love.

ACKNOWLEDGMENTS

No achievement in business or life happens without the support of our family, friends, and colleagues. I have been fortunate and lucky on all three counts. As a young professional, it was Jerry Yaros who believed in me and gave me my first break in the financial services industry.

It was my friendship with Steven Linden that led us to create Prestige Planning Group (now Prestige Wealth Management Group) in 1994, and it was the unwavering support of my family, friends, and colleagues that sustained me while our company grew in size and reputation.

A great deal of appreciation is reserved for the clients of PWMG who encouraged and motivated me to write this book so that I could share the principles that have allowed them to reach their life's goals and dreams.

Last, but certainly not least, a project like this requires a tremendous amount of support from the staff of PWMG. My dearest thanks go to Mark Andraos, John DeAngelo, Steven Fox, Linda Ialacci, Tom McCabe, Alyssa McMahon, Ken Paul, and Lisa Pro. In addition to the research and content, they contributed to the book. They have been responsive and resourceful as they reviewed chapters and made careful and thoughtful edits. They performed tirelessly while creating the best budgeting tool on the market exclusively for this book. I would also like to express my thanks and appreciation to my fearless editor, Mark Morrow. Thank you for all your words of encouragement and guidance throughout this rewarding project.

Finally, I'd like to thank and acknowledge the current and past employees at PWMG for focusing on our valuable clients and delivering on our strategic objective by making a positive and impactful difference in our clients' lives.

CHAPTER 1

Don't Underestimate How Long You Will Live

In This Chapter

▶ Making the Retirement Decision

▶ Mapping Out a Lifestyle You Can Afford

▶ Assessing Retirement Expenses and Income

▶ Planning Your Working-Life Exit

Planning for your retirement is a challenging job that requires people to make a reasonable guess about what might happen over the next 30 or so years. That's a tall order. But does retirement planning really need to be that magical or daunting?

Not really, especially if you stop focusing on the hundreds of details for a moment, step back, and survey the big picture. From this stress-free vantage point, retirement is a pretty straightforward job; simply put, planning for your retirement is just the wise allocation of two finite resources—time and money.

One of the resources—time—is absolutely finite. The other resource— money—is a finite resource as well, but thankfully, it's something we do have some control over.

Deadly Mistake #1

Outliving Your Savings

Living "Forever"

We often joke about living forever or never dying when the topic of mortality comes up in conversation. The quip is always good for a chuckle, but here's something to think about. If you're in reasonably good health, there's a chance you'll blow right past your 85th birthday and be around to see 90 candles on your birthday cake. That's great news if you're financially secure and in good health. The news is bad if you arrive at your 90th birthday and you can't pay for your basic living expenses.

Thinking About Your Retirement

Few people spend a great deal of time thinking about retirement, especially in the early years. When you're 24, the subject of retirement—and aging in general—is just laughable. By the time we are 34 or so with a mortgage and family commitments, retirement begins to lose its humorous edge—almost. After all, retirement from this vantage point is still 30 years away so planning can still wait until another day.

In our 40s and early 50s, retirement's event horizon seems perilously close. Still, many of us find a reason to put off taking action. We blame our current financial concerns (kids in college, other debt, and expenses), but promise to take up the question in earnest next year. Still, we find ourselves chuckling at work or at a neighborhood gathering when the topic of retirement is mentioned. Inevitably, someone (maybe you) will provide the punch line to any conversation about retiring; "Retirement, are you kidding? That's never going to happen."

The unfortunate fact about this gallows humor is that for many people the joke that they'll need to work forever or until they die is much closer to reality than they imagine. The fact is, millions of Americans will face financial difficulty during their retirement. But like most personal and even financial fixes, avoiding this fate is just a matter of deciding to take action.

Start With the Big Picture

Imagine you're building a house from the ground up. You likely know from the start that your house will be a one- or two-story structure with three or four bedrooms and an equal number of bathrooms. You also might be able to articulate your home's general layout and specific features of common areas like the kitchen.

At some point, you would meet with an architect and eventually a builder who would help match your financial resources with this big-picture vision. For most of us, this meeting means compromise on everything from kitchen appliances to the number and size of the bathrooms and bedrooms.

Retirement planning is a lot like this home construction scenario. It's a holistic process that forces us to align our ideal lifestyle vision with our current and projected financial resources. And similar to the home building process, it's a matter of choice, trade off, and compromise.

Current State of Retirement Planning

When Franklin Delano Roosevelt signed the Social Security Act in August of 1935, just surviving to your 65th birthday was pretty much a coin toss for both men and women. According to Social Security Administration statistics, only about 53 percent of the male population and 60 percent of the female population survived the high infant mortality rate prevalent at the time and then lived long enough to get a job, pay taxes, and get onto the Social Security roster. Today, more than 73 percent of men and 84 percent of women reach that status of tax-paying adulthood.[1]

In pure statistical terms, a 65-year-old male retiree today can expect to live about 19 more years or until age 84. Women can expect to live about 21 years beyond retirement or until age 86. Of course, these are just averages so the odds that you'll be celebrating your 85th or 87th birthday are pretty decent. In fact, about one out of every four of today's 65 year olds will live beyond age 90 and one out of 10 will live past age 95.[2]

And here's one more interesting (and perhaps concerning) aging statistic. A typical 65-year-old couple living today should at least consider the statistical probability that at least one of the two partners has an excellent chance to survive beyond the death of their spouse and live on to celebrate a 90th birthday.[3] Considering how dangerous it is just to be alive—getting run over by a bus, having a terminal disease, slipping in your bathtub, or falling down a flight of stairs—the assumption that *you*—the person reading this book—will be one of these threescore and thirty retirees is an amazing, but concerning, thought.

Why We're So Unprepared for Retirement

One major reason so many of us are unprepared for retirement is generational. The pre–baby boomer generation grew up in the shadow of the 1929 Great Depression. They experienced the effect of a failed economy. They watched banks and businesses close their doors and families lose their homes and farms. They experienced the awful, terrifying angst of being absolutely broke.

This experience defined a generation's attitude about money and saving for the future. It's also why most of us have seen our parents or grandparents carefully clean, fold, and store used aluminum foil, plastic wrap, and cottage cheese containers by the dozens. To this generation's way of thinking, you just never know what's going to happen so never, ever waste anything!

People don't plan to fail, they fail to plan.

The baby boom and successive generations have experienced no such angst about their future. Baby boomers in their 50s and 60s today grew up in an ever-expanding, post–World War II economy. And while this generation did experience the malaise-infused recession of the 1970s and the greed-stoked, boom-and-bust economic cycles in the 1980s and 1990s, these events hardly register on the hard-times meter when compared to the Great Depression. Even our six-year (and counting) crawl out of the effects of the Great Recession (a.k.a. the economic meltdown of 2008) fails to measure up.

No, the Great Depression and its particular set of historical and social circumstances (including the absence of any government-backed social safety net) is still the absolute benchmark for the total collapse of our economy.

Millennials, Generation X-ers and Y-ers, and the current generation coming of age are even further removed from the lessons of the Great Depression. These generations have known nothing but the expectation of plenty, and for the ones not so lucky, it's the world they aspire (and often expect) to join.

For the fortunate ones of these recent generations, they've had the opportunity to travel extensively. Many have lived in large, comfortable homes, driven late-model cars, and dined in fine restaurants. As members in good standing of our consumer society, they spend freely (often on credit) and save little, trusting a vague notion that it will all somehow work out in the end.

For some, this assumption will work out just fine, especially those with significant inheritances from their hardworking and successful Depression Era parents and grandparents. For those without such an endowed safety net, it's likely to be a rough ride without the financial discipline of a retirement plan.

Pensions and 401(k)s

When the "greatest generation" began retiring in the late 1970s and early 1980s, their loyal service (often to a single company) was rewarded with a generous pension and perhaps even access to post-retirement healthcare services. In 1970, 45 percent of all private-sector workers were still covered by a pension plan, according to the Employee Benefit Research Institute.[4] But by the 1980s, that long-term commitment to the individual employee began to shift as the actuarial reality of increasing lifespans and an ever-expanding retiree pool began to strain the resources of generous company pension plans.

In response, Congress passed the Revenue Act of 1978. The legislation provided the legal underpinning to support the concept of deferring income tax on retirement savings. Then in 1980, Ted Benna, a benefits consultant for the Johnson & Johnson Company, used the law to create the first 401(k) plan. A year later, the Internal Revenue Service issued a rule that allowed employees to fund 401(k) plans through salary reductions, and soon large companies, such as PepsiCo and Honeywell, began offering the benefit to their employees. By 1996, 401(k) assets topped $1 trillion. As of 2014, 401(k) assets exceed $3.5 trillion.[5]

Positive and Negative Sides of a 401(k)

Clearly, 401(k) plans enable millions to retire comfortably. These plans have largely replaced defined pension plans. Still, a 401(k) plan alone is not a replacement for a traditional pension plan. Company-matching policies for these retirement accounts vary widely, and they don't really compare to the pension plans of a generation ago because many of these traditional plans also included some form of healthcare coverage.

That's why every retiree's budget plan must include a line item for unanticipated health expenses and another line item for long-term care costs that exceed those provided by Medicare or private insurers. Here are a few considerations about investing in these plans:

Positive

▶ Employer-provided 401(k) plans allow you to control how much money is deferred (up to IRS and company plan maximums) and where your money is invested. Usually participants choose from a menu of investment options that include large cap (companies with a market capitalization value of more than $10 billion) and small cap (companies with a market capitalization between $300 million and $2 billion as well as international funds including emerging market funds.). Fast-moving technology-related companies are also offered as investment options through sector funds, as well as investments in low-risk bonds. As the owner of the fund, you get to choose the allocation percentages for each investment type.

Negative

▶ Investment freedom is a two-edged sword. You bear the responsibility for the success of your investment choices. Companies large enough to have a 401(k) plan work hard to ensure employees have access to basic investment training and advice. But the fact is that most participants make these decisions—if they pay attention at all—based on standard risk and time line calculations offered by the sponsoring company. That's a risky way to invest your retirement funds. For example, consider the effect on your 401(k) if you had allocated 95 percent of your portfolio's value to high-risk/high-return stocks in the technology sector right before the technology bubble blew up in 1999. Remember, whenever your investments suffer high losses, it's very difficult to make back the loss. For example, if your investments lost 80 percent in value it would take a 400 percent positive gain just to get even with your former position.

Good News / Bad News

Retirement planning today is certainly more challenging than it was a generation ago, but the good news outweighs the bad:

▶ *Bad News* – Yes, most companies no longer provide generous pension benefits to employees. But remember: most of these employees only collected these benefits for only 10 to 12 years due to shorter lifespans at the time.

▶ *Good News* – Your life expectancy beyond retirement has increased significantly. You have a good chance to live these extra years in better health. Yes, you'll have to be proactive about your own retirement planning, but if you plan wisely, you will have the money to spring for your 90th birthday celebration and pay the monthly fees at your comfortable assisted-living facility.

Creating Your Retirement Vision

A generation ago, most Americans had lower expectations for their post-retirement years. They generally took advantage of America's ever-expanding national road system and used their modern reliable cars to discover the land they had sacrificed to save. However, many baby boomers grew up taking full advantage of the unprecedented opportunity to travel nationally and internationally.

These same well-traveled retirees now plan on continuing their travel or re-engaging with a lifelong passion that was shelved while they climbed the corporate ladder or ran their own business. For this generation, retirement planning is more about the narrowing of choices, prioritizing what is fulfilling, and deciding what is affordable.

Despite all of the possibility—especially for the financially secure—some of our clients have great difficulty transitioning to retirement. Sometimes the difficulty stems from the loss of familiar workday routines and interacting with well-liked colleagues. Other clients miss careers that provided a tangible sense of self-worth and meaning for their lives. But on balance, most of our clients are ecstatic about retirement and fully embrace the opportunities of life with an open daily schedule.

A Day in Retirement

Later in this book, you'll get a chance to come face to face with the reality of making hard choices about your retirement vision, but for now just focus on the first day of your retirement. What would you be doing, thinking about, or planning for on that first day? Would you be training for a sporting event (a foot or bike race, perhaps)? Or do you imagine yourself getting up early, firing up your motorcycle or putting the top down in a classic convertible roadster from the 1960s, and heading out for the open road?

Envisioning a typical day or perfect day in retirement is a really good way to start the planning process. Try to start at the beginning of the day. What time do you get up? What do you do next? Do you make coffee? Do you go to the gym at 8:30 a.m. and secretly chuckle at the fact that you don't have a schedule to keep? If you're lucky enough to live near your grandchildren, might you imagine making a surprise visit?

You get the idea. Really think about how you'd interact with your new life. Imagine different scenarios based on time, affordability, or what your health will allow. If you feel overwhelmed by the possibilities and can easily imagine many ways to fill your day, then you're on the right track.

Other "Retirement" Pathways

Of course, not everyone works until they retire at the traditional age of 65. Some of our clients decide to retire in phases and step down from high-pressure corporate jobs to become a consultant for themselves or another firm. For many, shifting away from 10- to 12-hour workdays and moving toward a more reasonable and relaxed schedule is liberating. Other clients I've advised view consulting as a way to keep busy and at the same time ensure enough income to avoid the confines of living within a strict spending budget.

Where Do You Want To Live?

Most of us will stay in our current home after retirement, especially if the mortgage is paid. That's actually a smart strategy, at least in the short term, even if you do anticipate moving at some point. If there's no pressing reason to move, then take your time and make a reasoned and financially sound decision.

Below is a sampling of key questions to answer when discussing the desire to move:

▶ Will you keep your current home? How will you handle upkeep and maintenance? Would your life be easier if your house was smaller and you had less property to maintain?

▶ Is your house suitable for someone with limited mobility, i.e., one- or two-story construction? Would it be possible to reconfigure your home for single-floor living if necessary?

▶ Would you consider selling your home and renting a home to accommodate special needs?

▶ Is building a retirement-friendly home a possibility?

▶ How do you feel about moving into an active adult (55 years old and above) community?

▶ Are you considering relocating to a popular retirement location such as Florida, Arizona, or Nevada? If so:
  • Does the new community offer an acceptable level of quality medical care in close proximity to your new home?

From Our Practice...
Inflation Matters

The long-term effect of inflation on retirement savings always surprises my clients. It's just hard to imagine how someone with a steady, predictable retirement income stream and fixed expenses would suddenly be unable to pay their bills.

I had a client who had retired in 1984 with a $3,000 monthly pension and a fully paid healthcare plan that didn't even require copayments. On the face of it, you'd think this individual had a fantastic benefits package; and certainly, my client had a pension plan that's unheard of today. Unfortunately, the plan did not include an inflation adjustment clause so the pension paid the same fixed monthly amount no matter the current economic condition.

So, as time went by—and even with the modest inflation we'd had since the client's retirement—the pension's purchasing power was slowly reduced by inflation (still around 4 percent a year) until one day my client could no longer afford his lifestyle. In fact, my client would need a pension of $9,730 in 2014 just to match his $3,000 per month pension that served him well in 1984. Sadly, the net effect was that my client had outlived this savings. Ultimately, we had to sell his home just to meet retirement expenses and to maintain a positive cash flow.

- Will residents have similar interests? How many residents are close to your age? Visit during the months of November through May when a greater sampling of residents will be in their homes.

- Does the thought of spending your days with older people in a 55 and older community sound depressing?

▶ Are you considering buying a retirement home? Clearly, this is not an option for everyone, but even if the idea of traveling between homes sounds exotic, it may not make financial sense. Here are some general notes for your consideration:

  - How much time do you want to spend in your second home during the year?

  - Have you really calculated the costs of a second home: maintenance, community fees, paying for year-round utility services, lawn services, and other unexpected expenses of home ownership?

  - Have you compared the costs of renting a home for three months with the costs of owning a second home? You'll likely discover that renting is cheaper in most cases.

Calculating Expenses and Income

Despite a lifetime of direct experience with the third immutable rule of life, "everything costs more than you think," we still desperately cling to the notion that expenses will somehow be significantly lower after we retire.

Unfortunately, just like death and taxes, this reality of life does not change. That's why retirement planning is so essential. Without a plan and a realistic budget, your retirement years will be more *struggling to live* than living and enjoying life. The next chapter will help you make specific plans, but for now, here are some general thoughts and beginning steps.

Expenses

Most of us manage to underestimate the essentials of living on retirement budgets: food, shelter, clothing, and medical costs. But these budget line items don't compare with how much we underestimate the cost of having fun, i.e., vacations and other entertainment. After all, when you retire, every day is Saturday! Here are some key notes about the cost of fun and how to plan for these expenses:

▶ *It's Your Dime:* When you plan how much you'll spend on vacations and entertainment, remember that you are responsible for the full cost. If you traveled for your job and you used your frequent flyer miles to supplement these expenses, this perk ends with your job. Perhaps your former job allowed you to add vacation days at the end of your business travel days. If so, that perk is gone as well.

▶ *Other Vacation and Travel Considerations*
- What kind of travel do you like? Are you planning mostly domestic travel, or is international (Europe, Asia, tropical islands) your preference?

- Will you take short, mini-vacations near your home to visit friends, family, or grandchildren?

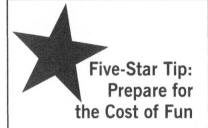

Five-Star Tip: Prepare for the Cost of Fun

Most of us underestimate what it costs to live after retirement. Part of the reason for our cost miscalculation is directly related to time. When we're working and rearing our children, time is in short supply. After retirement, every day suddenly feels like a Saturday. That means you'll likely travel more, dine out more, entertain more, watch more movies, and go to more cultural events. All are great activities, but when the costs are added up, it should come as no surprise that the costs you projected for travel and entertainment doubles or even triples.

- Do you plan to fund family trips that you'll take with your children and grandchildren?

- Do you plan more restaurant dining, or will you be entertaining your friends at home?

Retirement Contingency Planning

If the 2008 economic collapse taught us anything, it's the simple lesson to be prepared for anything. That's why I firmly believe in contingency planning that prepares you to handle unexpected expenses such as long-term healthcare and the inevitable swings in the economy. Here are some key just-in-case questions to ask yourself as you prepare to retire:

- How will I earn additional income if I lose a significant portion of my pension or investment portfolio?

- What are my marketable skills? Is consulting a possibility? Should I maintain certifications or licenses, and maintain work connections?

- Do I have a skill that might be turned into a part-time or even a full-time business (e.g., woodworking, event planning, technical skill training)?

You should at least investigate alternative income possibilities before you retire. Your skills and expertise may be more valuable than you think, and knowing that you have a what-if plan will make your retirement even more enjoyable. For example, you might work or consult a few hours per month to keep your skills up to date and relevant as part of your retirement contingency plan.

What's Next and Wrap Up

Chapter 2 is designed to help you leave behind any notion that your finances will be more predictable after you retire. It examines the many risks posed by financial surprises as we age and offers ways to meet this challenge. Finally, the chapter presents a comprehensive budgeting tool you can use to begin planning for your own retirement.

Here's a recap of the key information presented in this chapter:

▶ Sure, no one lives forever, but if you don't have enough financial resources to enjoy a long life and good health, then it just might feel that way.

▶ Think of retirement planning like building a house. Start with the big picture before worrying about the details.

▶ You, the person reading this book, have a very good chance of living past your 85th birthday and into your 90s. Be prepared!

▶ If you have a 401(k), it's your responsibility to make sure your retirement assets are secure, so monitor its performance and seek out reliable advice.

▶ Imagining a day in retirement will help you construct a retirement plan you can live with and afford.

▶ If you plan to change your living situation, think carefully and don't take hasty action. After all, once you've retired you'll have plenty of time to make the right decision.

▶ Expenses rise to meet income. Don't be surprised by the high cost of retirement.

Be Realistic About Retirement Expenses

In This Chapter

▶ The Wisdom of No Debt

▶ Job Loss and Other Unanticipated Financial Surprises

▶ Healthcare Disasters

▶ Home Location

Just about everything we do in life ends up costing more than our original estimate. Whether it's the deafening "cha-ching" heard as we pull out our credit card to pay for a major car repair during a family vacation or the barely audible, but still annoying, "cha-ching" of a $25 parking ticket, we're constantly reminded that a significant number of life's expenses are "not in the budget." So why, given this extensive experience and a lifetime of daily reminders, would we assume this rule no longer applies in retirement?

If this chapter accomplishes anything, I hope it will help you leave behind any notion that your finances will be more predictable after you retire. The fact is, your expenses are even less predictable in retirement because the frequency of the

Deadly Mistake #2

Failing to Plan

financial surprises and risks posed by these unantici-pated expenses just increase as we age. More significantly, because retirement means you no longer have a continuing stream of predictable income to pay for these unbudgeted expenses, every dime you spend today paying for these costs means you'll have that much less money to spend on tomorrow's unplanned cash drains.

The good news is that designing a near foolproof retirement plan that insulates you from most of life's potential financial catastrophes is entirely possible. Whether it's weathering extreme periods of market volatility, paying for the cost of long-term care, or funding a big-ticket home maintenance project such as a roof replacement, the best plan of action is setting up and adhering to a comprehensive budget.

Later, we will review how to build a budgeting plan that provides financial security, but before we get to these details, let's examine how most Americans prepare financially for retirement, and more importantly how, when, and why they accumulate debt.

The Wisdom of No Debt

According to a paper presented at the 15th Annual Joint Meeting of the Retirement Research Consortium, a little more than half (55%) of the American population between the ages of 55 and 64 currently carry a mortgage. And even for Americans between the ages of 65 and 74 that percentage drops only slightly to 50 percent. Surprisingly, the study reports that about 30 percent of those in this 65- to 74-year-old age group also carry credit card debt.[1]

This statistic makes two points. The first is that, at least according to my own financial management preferences, Americans are carrying too much debt. The second is that just because you have debt doesn't mean you are facing a bleak financial future. Clearly, no single approach to retirement planning fits all financial circumstances. However, if I've learned anything during my 30-plus years in this business it's that no one ever got into financial trouble because they had no debt.

And it's that point of view that informs the advice I give to most of my clients; you should carry as little debt as possible into retirement. Here are a few reasons why I believe this is the right financial management strategy:

1. Debt directly drains your fixed retirement assets.

2. Debt presents a major risk to your retirement portfolio's overall health and available cash flow, especially when tax rules require a withdrawal without regard to the market environment.

3. Debt creates worry and if you are debt free it just stands to reason that you'll worry less and get a better night's sleep.

Debt for the Boomers

Unfortunately, the current wave of retirees may have little leeway in their decision about carrying debt into retirement. According to a recent Retirement Research Consortium report, the boomer generation generally bought bigger, more expensive homes and freely indulged in home equity and credit card borrowing to afford their lifestyle.[2]

Certainly the 2008 economic meltdown highlighted the unsustainability of leveraging personal debt, but this late-arriving insight won't change the fact that millions of baby boomers are saddled with the prospect of managing more retirement debt than any previous generation. Because an essential strategy of long-term

Why Being Mortgage Free During a Market Crash Makes Sense

Here's an example of how a 50 percent decline in the market would affect your monthly cash flow.

If the value of your portfolio BEFORE the market crash was $1 million, AFTER the crash it would be worth only $500,000.

Now assume that $30,000 of your annual cash flow is supplied by your portfolio. Here's the direct effect on your financial position:

Before Market Crash
$30,000 = 3 percent of your portfolio's value
($30,000/$1 million)

After Market Crash
$30,000 = 6 percent of your portfolio's value
($30,000/$500,000)

retirement planning focuses on lowering expenses, as the iconic Grateful Dead album clearly spells out to its aging boomer fans, there might be "trouble ahead" for many of these future retirees.[3]

Mortgage Debt

So why would I feel so strongly about debt? As a financial planner, it's my job to think about the financial effect of every decision made by my clients and to advise them if their financial position is improving or getting worse. For some, keeping a home mortgage into retirement is the best decision because it allows them to remain in a lower tax bracket if they continue to claim a mortgage interest deduction when they file their taxes.

For example, if you can earn a rate of return of, let's say, 5 percent on your assets and your mortgage rate is only 3 percent, then the growth of your assets is sufficient enough to cover the interest payments on your debt. Vice versa: if you're not earning sufficient returns to cover the interest rate on your mortgage, you may be better off paying off your mortgage.

So if the market experiences a 50 percent drop in value as it did during the 2008 economic crash, your monthly mortgage payment might suddenly consume twice as much of your portfolio's monthly financial performance. In practical terms, if your mortgage payment before the crash was 3 percent of your monthly cash flow, that same portfolio after the crash—now worth only half of its original value—would consume 6 percent of your monthly cash flow just to generate the same amount of money. And that percentage jump (from 3 to 6 percent) is where the long-term trouble begins and your risk of running out of money in your retirement years begins. (See sidebar on previous page for example.)

This leveraged debt principle is demonstrated regularly in the highly volatile real estate market. Some of our clients use leverage very successfully and rarely get into trouble with debt, but the fact is some of our most financially stable clients don't use debt to build wealth. These clients take on debt to buy a property if needed, but they pay that debt off as soon as possible. For these investors, full, debt-free ownership of rental properties means they always have a positive cash flow. In good times, a real estate investor whose rental income portfolio is based on debt might appear successful, but like all pyramid schemes, failure—usually in response to one of our economy's regularly occurring market correction cycles—is inevitable. And when these market corrections happen, the most debt-leveraged investors have no choice but to declare bankruptcy.

Of course, decisions about debt varies by circumstance. If a client had investments worth $1 million, lived in a $1 million home, and carried a 3.75 percent fixed mortgage rate on a $300,000 home loan, I would likely advise them to pay off the loan before they retired, if no other tax or investment strategy were involved. Or, if this client had fewer assets and a high-value home, I might advise them to sell the home, downsize to a smaller home, and preserve the remaining cash for retirement expenses. An important note here is that the federal tax law allows you to avoid paying capital gains on the sale of a primary home up to $500,000 for married individuals and $250,000 for single persons.

I have a bias toward positive cash flow, and sometimes that might seem counterintuitive. For example, if that same client with a 3.75 percent mortgage rate also held a five-year, high quality, AA-rated bond returning 1.85 percent, I'd advise the client to pay off the mortgage using the bond. A client following this strategy would create a positive cash flow of around 2 percent (the difference between the bank's mortgage interest rate and the bond's yield).

Many of our clients make the perfectly logical assumption that they should keep their mortgages to take advantage of the mortgage tax deduction. While that sometimes does make financial sense, depending on your income tax situation, you might not be able to take the full mortgage deduction. In these cases, the difference between how much mortgage interest you pay annually and the amount you can claim as a tax deduction might turn out to be a minimal amount. In any case, my general rule of thumb is to advise my clients to pay off their mortgage and take a nice vacation every year with the savings.

Even if a client has more assets and investments, I often give the same debt-free retirement advice. In fact, one of our highest net worth wealth clients recently retired, and although their investments would have serviced their remaining mortgage debt without affecting the client's long-term financial outlook, we decided that paying off

Home Equity Car Purchase Example

Using a home equity loan to buy a car is an acceptable financial strategy in some circumstances. Just make sure that you limit the terms of the loan so that it is paid off within five years. Because many home equity loans don't require you to pay off the loan for up to 20 years, your $30,000 car might end up costing much more than you realize. Here's how your $30,000 car might end up costing you more than $45,550:

Purchase Price - $30,000
Home Equity Rate - $4.5%
Monthly Payment - $189.79
(Term - 20 Years)
Final Cost - $45,550

Of course, interest rates are at a historic low point, so it's possible to get 0%, 1%, or 2% on a new car loan. But even these low rates don't necessarily mean that you should sign up for these loans. Sometimes, paying cash (even from your investment portfolio) might make sense if outright purchase means a high cash back reward or a significantly lower price on the car. The point is, before you make any investment consider all potential financial implications, positive or negative, of your decision.

the mortgage and all other debts was the right decision. The client made that decision because he and his family valued the liberating emotional feeling of being debt-free. The bottom line is that my experience with this client and hundreds of other clients is that those who enter retirement with this no-debt mindset enjoy less stressful marriages and lives after retirement. You just can't put a price on that!

Home Equity Loans

Prior to the 2008 economic meltdown the value of home equity originations in the United States was $430 billion as compared to $111 billion in 2013 (up more than 30 percent from the year before).[4] That's because millions of Americans thought of their homes as just inexhaustible ATMs that would allow them to buy expensive cars, fund over-the-top home renovations, or purchase vacation homes. Of course, we all know how that turned out.

During the home equity frenzy, we advised our clients to carefully consider the financial effect of home equity loans, especially for those building a retirement plan. It's not that I'm opposed to home equity loans. Clearly, many people use their home equity in careful and judicious ways to pay for needed home renovation projects or for a life emergency that requires an immediate cash infusion.

In fact, I often recommend establishing a home equity line of credit to pay for these unforeseen calamities of life. Establishing this emergency fund is actually an important step for someone who relies on cash flow from investment account distributions or for those without pensions or other liquid cash reserves equal to six months to two years of expenses.

What I don't recommend to any of our clients very often is using a home equity loan to buy a car. Here's why. Many consumers maintain a home equity loan balance for years, often just making the minimum interest payment on the loan each month. What these consumers don't realize is that the accumulated interest charges over a period of 10, 15, or 20 years means that they may end up paying up to 50 percent more for the car (see sidebar). And this extra cost may be for a car that they long ago donated to charity or now use to haul bags of dirt back from Home Depot. Again, I'm not opposed to using a home equity loan to purchase a car or for any other reason, but I do recommend that if you do use your home equity to limit the loan terms to five years and pay it off.

Credit Card Debt

You might assume that credit card debt hardly deserves a mention in a book focused on smart retirement financial strategies. Clearly, we all know it's a bad financial strategy to accumulate any credit card debt you can't pay off at the end of each month. But a surprising number of Americans carry large credit card debt.

According to the website NerdWallet.com, whose statistics are often quoted by the *New York*

Five-Star Tip: Monitor Credit Habits of Your Children

You might think that paying off credit card debt is an obvious financial strategy, but many otherwise smart people get into trouble with high credit card debt. And before the 2008 economic meltdown, the potential for trouble extended to kids in college with little or no credit history.

I remember going to a football game when my son was in college, and at every entrance I saw credit card companies handing out applications to the kids along with towels, beer mugs, and coolers. Of course, you know what happened. Some of these kids graduated with tremendous credit card debt!

So do some financial oversight with your kids in college with a credit card by letting them know you'll be monitoring their credit card spending.

Times, CNN, and other media outlets, the average U.S. household credit card debt as of November 2013 stood at $15,112 based on an analysis of Federal Reserve statistics and other government data.[5] While this debt level is lower than the $19,000 per household level recorded in 2009, the current level is still surprising and for some it's an absolute threat to their retirement security.

Part of the reason for this debt is directly traceable to the 2008 financial crisis, but a more significant reason for this debt are social, economic, and educational factors that encourage immediate acquisition of anything we want – unlike previous generations who put off purchases until they could truly afford the things they wanted.

Unanticipated Expenses and Other Spending Surprises

If we knew what would happen over the next 30 or 40 years—or could confidently assume what would happen—then retirement planning would be simple. Unfortunately, that world doesn't exist. Stuff happens and so we must be prepared to deal with it. Here are a few examples from my list of unanticipated circumstances:

Job Loss or Early/Phased Retirement

Millions of Americans experienced one of life's most devastating unanticipated events as a result of the 2008 financial crisis—the loss of a job. This job loss was particularly devastating for those in their 50s and 60s. Some of these workers—the more fortunate ones—were offered generous severance packages and just retired early or became independent consultants. Others who lost their jobs (those leaving with minimal or no severance packages) have spent the last five years underemployed, unemployed, or preparing for a late-life career change while they slowly depleted their retirement savings.

But regardless of the reasons for retirement—forced or voluntary—the most important question to ask at any of life's crossroads is, *What's next?* While I don't diminish the terrible effect of job loss or a reverse in fortunes, a positive attitude unleashes creativity and allows us to see possibilities. If that means changing careers or working longer than we anticipated, then it's a lot easier to do when you're looking forward to new possibilities.

On the other side of the coin are clients who retire and are lost without their routine or the trappings of power and authority. Money may not be the problem, but feeling unplugged from the world can be just as disheartening. For these clients, I encourage a second consulting career or suggest engaging in a consuming passion.

I have one client in his 80s who works at a Home Depot, not because he particularly needs the money (although it is a nice benefit), but because he says it keeps him engaged in life. Another client wanted to buy a large boat after he retired, and when we looked at the financial drain, the client decided to start a second consulting career to fund his passion. No matter the circumstances, the bottom line is that thriving in retirement is all about staying engaged with what's next and doing what is necessary to keep moving forward.

> **Average Cost of a Wedding**
>
> According to the website *costofwedding.com*, the average cost of a wedding is $25,656. However, most couples spend between $19,242 and $32,070. Of course, the website notes that these wedding statistics don't include the cost for a honeymoon.[6]

Wedding

Traditionally, the father of the bride pays for the wedding, so if you raised two daughters then this expense might be one of the anticipated expenses in your retirement budget. But what if you don't have any girls in your family? Should you plan to fund at least some of your son's wedding expenses? Absolutely! Sharing wedding expenses between parents of the bride and groom is a common practice today. So, if the bride's financial circumstances won't allow for full or even equitable sharing of wedding expenses, then you might have to chip in more than you ever anticipated to the wedding party.

When I have this discussion with my clients, particularly clients with boys, I advise them to set aside a defined amount for these shared wedding expenses in a separate account just in case. If the funds are not ultimately needed, the cash is an unanticipated windfall for your portfolio.

The Boomerang Effect by the Numbers

We all know that a huge number of recent college graduates are currently living with their parents, but how many?

A 2013 study commissioned by the *Atlantic* magazine and carried out by the Pew Research Center revealed that 61% more college-educated 18- to 34-year-olds were living with their families during 2011 than were doing so in 2001.

Interestingly, the data also revealed that the boomerang effect has affected all young people whether or not they went to college.[7]

Boomerang Children

In addition to sending millions of working adults out in the streets to look for work, the 2008 financial meltdown and the following five years of slow recovery has meant that recent college graduates had a tough time finding work. And even when these graduates did find jobs, the pay for the jobs (often an entry-level job and often not related to their majors) was inadequate at best. This economic dynamic has resulted in a whole new generation of *boomerang* children who have returned to their parents' homes after college to save money while they wait out the recession.

If you are still working when your college graduate son or daughter shows up at your doorstep, the unanticipated expense is not likely to affect your household budget that much. But if you're retired and living on investment income, then taking your children back will require some financial and lifestyle adjustments.

Beyond these obvious financial adjustments, I always advise my clients to think through the potential emotional effect of their open-door generosity, specifically, using the experience to enable and not disable their children. Here are some points based on my years of client experiences that I believe will *enable* your children and positively affect the financial health of your portfolio and future success of your children:

▶ If your child is working—no matter how small the paycheck—ask them to pay some level of rent.

▶ Give them regular household chores such as cooking and cleaning.

▶ Don't let them stay indefinitely and take advantage of your "free" living arrangement, especially when they get a job that pays a decent wage.

▶ Make them live by your standards and rules. For the most part, the phrase "my house, my rules" should still apply.

▶ Resist returning to old roles, i.e., don't do their laundry or make their beds.

▶ Help them plan and budget to be independent after they leave your home.

Paying rent might seem a less-than-generous way to treat a child forced to come home as a result of the worst financial downturn in a generation, but the lesson of paying rent (even a small amount) is that shelter will not always be free so get used to it.

My two boys had to do their own laundry and other household chores. Asking them to do that simple chore meant that when they went to college we didn't get phone calls asking how to do laundry. We enabled them with the knowledge and expectation that no one was going to do it for them.

Even if you enjoy having your children around, you're not doing them any favors by letting them stay at home and, in some cases, live off your hard-earned portfolio indefinitely. When your boomerang children can afford to move out, send them on their way with your blessing and good wishes.

Expanded and Blended Families

It's just a fact of life that spouses sometimes die or marriages fail and the result is some level of blended or expanded family circumstances. While these new family arrangements may be rewarding and enriching to your life, they can also complicate your financial and retirement planning.

For example, if you're a man in your late 40s, 50s, or even early 60s and marry a younger woman eager to start a family, you'll need to consider the long-term financial consequences. Remember, no matter how you calculate it, raising a child through age

18 will cost most middle class families at least $250,000. So, you'll likely have to work until you're 70 or 75 to pay the bills.[8]

Remarrying due to the death of a spouse or divorce has other often-overlooked potential expenses. For example, you may have to contribute to the wedding expenses of your stepson or stepdaughter, or you might incur additional college expense or other unanticipated expenses due to your new blended family circumstance. You might have to take on the debt of a new spouse or even pay for vacations that might include a larger extended family. In addition, you should consider if your spouse is younger, you have to work longer because your portfolio will need to last many more years than you would with a spouse of the same age.

Parent & Grandparent Costs

Parents are generally very happy to help their children in any reasonable way, and some ways may even be tax deductible. But as I pointed out earlier about letting your children move back home, your generosity has the power to either enable or disable your children.

First, it is important to be clear about money expectations in your retirement plan. If you intend to give one of your children $10,000 to help them make a down payment on a house, don't call it a loan if in fact it is a gift. This clarity helps set boundaries.

Second, if you decide to co-sign a mortgage loan with your son or daughter (something I don't recommend very often), then make sure your child is paying their mortgage obligation on time so that your credit won't be damaged. This level of caution, even with your own children, is more a decision about managing the downside risk. And if you want to loan a significant amount of money to one of your children but you really do need the money to fund your long-term retirement plans, then don't loan the money. It really should be a simple yes or no answer.

I will offer a number of gifting strategies for children and grandchildren later in this book, but in general, helping out your grandchildren with college expenses, providing cash for the down payment on a car or house, or any other worthwhile expense is a legitimate way to help out those you love if you can afford it. But remember, be clear about why you're providing financial help to your children or grandchildren and always make sure your generosity enables their success.

Watching your children grow up and have children of their own is a fulfilling and happy experience, but if your children live on the West Coast and you live on the East Coast just keeping your grandparent connection alive can get expensive. Not only does this unanticipated expense include travel, but you have to factor in the cost of special-occasion gifts—birthdays and holidays. If you can afford it, then you'll need to consider the expense of setting aside money you want to contribute to your grandchildren's college fund. While these and other expenses might seem obvious when you see them in print, it's surprising how many retirement plans don't account for these expenses.

Sandwich Generation

A January 2013 report published by the Pew Research Center revealed that nearly 50 percent of adults in their 40s and 50s are at risk of supporting both of their parents and their own children; that is, they have a parent aged 65 or older and are either raising a young child or

Reverse Mortgages

A reverse mortgage allows you to get income from the equity you've built in your home. For some circumstances, a reverse mortgage makes sense. If this is something you are considering, you'll need to discuss this decision with a trusted financial expert who knows your financial situation.[9]

In general, you should watch out for the following downsides:

- **Bank charges:** you might be required to pay a fee of several thousand dollars or a certain percentage of the loan to the bank.

- **High processing fees:** you might have to pay home appraisal fees and other fees associated with selling a home.

- **Loss of family home:** if keeping the family home is important, acquiring the home back from the bank may not be affordable.

- **Medicaid benefits:** since eligibility for Medicaid depends on liquid resources, taking the income might affect eligibility.

- **Recall of mortgage:** sometimes homeowners are unaware of contract details and certain circumstances— missing tax payments or not keeping adequate insurance—might result in a bank recalling the loan.

financially supporting a child older than 18. Currently, about one in seven of these middle-aged adults (15%) are providing financial support to both of their aging parents and a child.[10]

Clearly, providing financial support to both of your parents and your children is an unanticipated expense that could have a serious effect on your retirement plans, not to mention your emotional life. According to the report, those with the responsibility to support both their children and parents are stressed emotionally and often worry about having enough money for their own retirement.

Healthcare Costs

According to US government statistics, the current average cost of assisted-living in the United States is $3,292 per month, while the average cost of a month's stay in a nursing home is $6,235.[11] And, depending on the state you live in, the cost for these services can easily double. That means even a five-year stay in an assisted-living facility will cost nearly $200,000, while five years in a nursing home will take a nearly $375,000 bite out of your retirement accounts. And that's an average! So how do you afford this cost when there's a very good chance that you'll live at least into your mid- to late 80s or perhaps even longer?

While many Americans purchase long-term care insurance, most of us don't and so this expense must be covered by investment returns and other assets. Although using a reverse mortgage on your home should be a strategy of last resort (see Reverse Mortgage sidebar), I recommend this option if it means living out your life with dignity at home. Another long-term funding option is to just sell your home outright and rent.

I had a client who had major surgery and a significant portion of the expenses were not covered by insurance. Once fully recovered, he and his wife sold their home, found a home to rent and used the money to finance the rest of their lives. They had a ball just living their lives to the fullest.

A 2013 Kaiser Family Foundation and Health Research Educational Trust survey revealed that an average family insurance plan costs the employer nearly $16,000 annually per employee. The average insurance premium cost for the employee is $4,565 per year.[12] Before passage of the Affordable Care Act (ACA) in 2012, individuals who bought insurance on the open market (usually a high-deductible plan) could expect to spend between $400 and $1,200 per month for coverage.[13]

The ultimate effect on the cost of healthcare that was heralded by the 2012 passage of President Obama's landmark legislation is still very much a matter of speculation. In fact, the deadline to sign up for coverage coincides with the publication date of this book.

Nevertheless, if the full promise of the ACA is achieved, it is possible that current and future retirees would indeed have a less financially burdensome healthcare bill. But for now, my advice would be to hope for the best outcome—better, less expensive healthcare for everyone—but prepare for a less rosy outcome. In the meantime, here are some early recommendations about the ACA:

▶ Shop on the healthcare exchange and compare policies.

▶ Compare coverage to what you had before (i.e., co-pays, deductibles).

▶ As the exchanges expand and improve, changing where you buy coverage might make sense so monitor the ACA carefully.

Loss of Executive Perks and Travel Rewards

One of the most overlooked, but easily anticipated new expense in retirement is the additional cost you'll incur due to the loss of perks associated with your job, particularly vacation and travel costs. If you've grown accustomed to some of your vacation air travel and lodging being paid for with reward or frequent flyer points accumulated due to job-related travel, then you'll need to consider this additional lifestyle cost. I have one client who continues to travel on reward points 10 years after he retired, but this is an unusual case. Most of us with these surplus reward miles are traveling on our own dime much sooner. Independent business owners who have grown accustomed to a significant portion of their car and travel expenses being legitimate tax-deductible expenses also have to add back these budget expense lines in their retirement budgets.

The point is, if you want to continue a certain level of pre-retirement travel and comfort, you'll need to anticipate these costs.

What's Next and Wrap Up

Chapter 3 will help you translate this chapter's retirement planning "what ifs" into the specifics of building a retirement budget.

Here's a recap of the key information presented in this chapter:

▶ Everything costs more than you anticipate—especially retirement—so plan accordingly.

▶ Retire with as little debt as possible. Remember, no one ever got into financial trouble because they had no debt.

▶ If possible, retire without a home mortgage and debt free.

▶ Be very cautious about using your home equity. If you do use it, make sure you limit the terms of the loan to as few years as possible to avoid the accumulation of long-term interest charges.

▶ Life is full of surprises. The best way to weather unanticipated events is by having a good attitude and always asking, "What's next?"

▶ Helping your children and grandchildren financially is an admirable gesture. Just make sure that everything you do for them enables their potential success in life.

▶ Healthcare is expensive—even with the still-evolving implementation of the Affordable Care Act—so plan your budget accordingly.

▶ Marriage and divorce later in life are common events, but the cost and consequences of these changes are often overlooked, especially the potential cost of having children later in life.

Create a Realistic Budget and Stick to It

In This Chapter

▶ Learn How Inflation Affects Budgeting

▶ Determine the True Cost of Living

▶ Budget for the Unexpected

▶ Celebrate Being a Smart Consumer

▶ Build a Budget on a Solid Foundation

Just the idea of creating a personal budget conjures up visions of being forced to live within unreasonable and miserly financial constraints. But creating a realistic retirement budget can be an *empowering* exercise that actually puts *you* in charge of achieving your life goals before and after retirement.

Without a careful accounting of your income and expenses, you won't know for sure if your month-long tour of wineries in Europe (or any other grand or even modest plan you might conjure up) is even possible, nor will you have any idea of the lifestyle changes needed to make your dream trip a reality. You can, of course, wing your finances and ignore important questions of long-term affordability, but

Deadly Mistake #3
Unrealistic Spending Expectations

at some point you'll have to confront a simple, but terrifying, question: "Will I be out of money?"

This chapter is designed to accomplish two goals: (1) to shift your views about maintaining a budget and (2) to reinforce an unsurprising, but often overlooked, retirement reality that everything will cost more than you might ever imagine. As I pointed out in Chapter 2, many expenses such as housing or potential taxes are easily anticipated. But it's the expenses you never thought would happen that wreak havoc with retirement savings.

Traditional Rainy-Day Scenarios

The standard rainy-day advice to maintain liquid assets (money market, certificates of deposits, traditional savings, or other assets that can be quickly converted to cash) equal to at least six months of your normal monthly expenses is a good baseline rule. But then, not everyone's financial situation is the same so the right level of liquid assets for you might be equal to 10 or 12 months of expenses, perhaps even up to 24 months.

So what are some typical unplanned expenses? Of course, you can easily imagine a few: replacing a car or a roof that suddenly needs replacing. But, as discussed in the last chapter, the biggest unanticipated budget buster is an uninsured or uncovered health crisis. Of course, there are other less dramatic ways of getting backed into a financial corner such as selling an equity position in a key investment at the wrong time or taking on too much debt.

The Silent Killer

Inflation is sometimes called the silent killer of your portfolio's value because it slowly eats away at your portfolio's purchasing power over a period of years without giving you any obvious red flags such as a sudden drop in value. Imagine yourself as the captain of a ship carrying an irreplaceable cargo of retirement savings. As a well-informed captain, you know that the Inflation Sea is a danger-

Inflation Variations Over the Last 20 Years

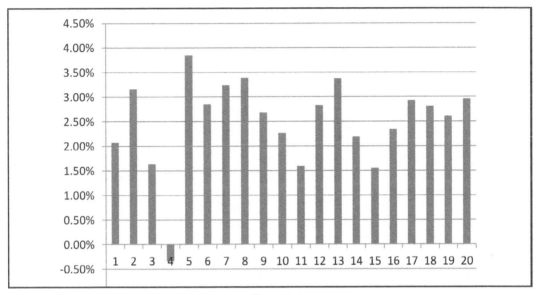

Figure 3.1

ous place. Ships that stay afloat are commanded by captains who understand the danger posed by declining value leaks down below as well as the financial storm clouds gathering on the horizon.

You might think this sailing analogy is a bit dramatic, but it's easy to demonstrate that failure to respect the power of inflation is very unwise.

Since 1926, inflation has averaged about 4 percent per year (it's actually 3.74 percent, but most financial planners use 4 percent to plan). In 1993, the rate of inflation was 2.9 percent, and in 1999 the rate dropped to 1.99 percent. In 2008, just at the start of the Great Recession, the inflation rate was 3.85 percent, and in 2013 it was pegged at 1.50 percent.[1] For a snapshot of inflation's variations over the last 20 years, see Figure 3.1. Of course, it's hard to appreciate how the inflation rate affects the value of the dollar by looking at a chart so let's go back in time and imagine the experience of buying a new car.

It's 1979 and you've decided to buy a new Mazda GLC—a popular brand at the time—so you walk into the local dealership and you're floored by the sticker price—$4,665. A quick calculation tells you that the price is just a little less than half your yearly salary, but you press on, make the deal, and agree to pay financing of $115 per month.

Today, just by adding in the effect of inflation alone, the same car would cost $15,949. If you'd like to see the effect of inflation on some of your own past purchases, visit USinflationCalculator.com.[2] By way of comparison, the median cost of a house in 1979 was $69,600; and the average cost of room, board, and tuition at a four-year public university was less than $2,500; and the cost of one year at a good private university was about $5,400.[3]

And here are some other interesting facts about the rate of inflation that you might not know. First, when the government calculates the rate of inflation, it does not include the cost of food and fuel. That might seem like an oversight, but the simple explanation is that the government considers these costs unstable. So, according to this logic, focusing on what we buy (shoes to wedding rings to medical care) provides a much more consistent snapshot of the economy.

While this may help economists with their economic predictions and market calculations, it ends up giving the rest of us an inaccurate picture of the true cost of living. That may be one reason that last year's 1.5 percent inflation felt more financially constrained than the numbers warranted.[4]

Estimated Monthly Expenses

If you've ever taken the time to add up the monthly expense for almost anything—groceries, Starbuck's coffee, lunch—the bottom-line expense was likely shocking. Even so, most of our clients were surprised to find during the retirement budget-planning process that their projected fixed and discretionary expenses will exceed their projected income, usually by a margin of between 20 and 25 percent. Some clients discover the underestimation is 40 or 50 percent. This pattern of underestimation holds true for both the high-paid executives used to meeting tight revenue and expense guidelines and those with less financial experience.

The reason for this underestimation is due to a phenomenon I call the "every day is Saturday" effect. That is, if you don't have a schedule or a job to worry about, you end up entertaining and traveling more *just because you can*, and that flexibility always requires more money.

For example, consider the expense of visiting your children or grandchildren. It's great if they live a short distance from your home, but what if they live 1,500 or 3,000 miles away. It's easy to imagine making three or four trips each year for events such as a christening, a birthday, or the holidays. It's just as easy to imagine that you'll spend $4,000 to $5,000 for each of these trips including the airfare, meals out, gifts, and other incidental costs. Add this expense up and that's $12,000 to $20,000 a year. Suddenly, your well-planned retirement cash flow is in serious trouble even before accounting for the rate of inflation.

I can give a real-life example of this expense scenario from my own life. I live in New Jersey, but my son and his wife live in California. They have a new child, and so for one reason or another my wife and I have been to the West Coast three times in the last six months. Of course, we're happy to make the trip, but there are some common expense realities revealed by all of this travel.

On one of these trips, we decided to visit friends who live in the Napa Valley region of Northern California so that added extra airfare from Southern to Northern California. My son happened to have a guest room, but if this had not been the case or some family dynamic or personal preference had prevented us from access to free lodging, the cost

Five-Star Tip: Establish a Fund for Expenses Not Covered by Insurance Claims

Set up a separate savings account for repairs and other improvements that might not be covered by your insurance policy.

These additional expenses can range from a few thousand dollars of extra expense (illustrated by a client's decision to add new kitchen cabinets to their insurance claim amount) to more devastating scenarios involving inadequate coverage for major damage and loss.

Many homeowners (and business owners) experienced extraordinary losses as a result of Hurricane Sandy in 2012. I recently had a conversation with a business owner who didn't have the proper insurance to protect an in-progress renovation of his business. The oversight resulted in bankruptcy for his formerly profitable business.

Five-Star Tip: Make a Bucket List

Like the popular movie, *The Bucket List*, make your own bucket list of what you want to accomplish with the rest of your life. Whether it's travel or education or a creative endeavor such as opening an art gallery, commit it to paper. Next, determine a plan of action that will allow you to check off the items on your list. It's a good idea for the couple to make separate lists, reach an agreement about the lists and then take turns on which trip gets priority.

Here are a few items on my list:

• Visit the Galápagos Islands.

• Spend some time in the Amazon rain forest.

• See all the US National Parks.

• Visit Alaska.

• Go to Oaxaca, Mayan ruins.

of a hotel would be just another expense tacked onto this scenario. Right now, my grandchildren are not old enough to insist on a trip to Disneyland, but special treats like this certainly add to the cost of a trip. Finally, the cost of restaurant meals adds to the total cost of a family trip. Sure, these special nights out are fun and meaningful, but over the course of a week or ten days, all that entertainment will cost way more than you anticipated.

Home Insurance Coverage

Americans pay an average of between $300 and $1,000 each year to insure their homes and possessions against potential losses (that's on the median price of a single-family home currently pegged at about $285,000).[5] We bear this expense to protect our homes and property against unforeseen disasters and expect our insurance carrier to pay for all replacement costs beyond our policy deductible. While this expectation is usually safe to make, sometimes a small home disaster such as water damage caused by a leaking refrigerator icemaker becomes an opening to do additional home improvement.

A few years ago, we had some water damage to our kitchen caused by this exact scenario—a leaking ice maker supply line. It's a common claim so our insurance company quickly settled and wrote a check to repair the damage. Unfortunately, my wife saw this as an opportunity to replace the kitchen cabinets and do some other upgrade work that greatly exceeded the payment our insurance agent handed us.

So the message here is clear. Whether it's the unanticipated cost of travel, a decision to go on a clothes and toy buying spree for your grandchildren, or turning a simple insurance claim into a full-scale home improvement project, plan on your actual expenses to outstrip your estimate.

Lifestyle Activities

Deciding on how you want to spend your retirement years should be a deliberate activity. This means engaging with your spouse or partner collaboratively to plan your new life. I always tell my clients to make a bucket list of the activities so that we can work together to determine how to fund these aspirations.

Some of my clients make separate lists and then work together to create a single list, while other clients work together from the beginning of the bucket list creation process. No matter the process, you'll avoid common conflict flashpoints by starting the list with this collaborative mindset and then extending it to include which bucket list item takes precedence during a given year, month, or quarter. My personal and client experience tells me that not only does this approach reduce stress and avoid conflict, but it often leads to surprising discoveries.

For example, a few years ago my wife insisted on a trip to Yosemite National Park in California, a bucket list item that was high on her list but not mine. I went along with the plan, and as it turned out, I rate this as one of our very best vacations. The one caveat to this compromise approach is to make sure the cost is equitable between the bucket list options you're comparing. A camping trip to the Adirondacks and a

The High Cost of Mickey Mouse

One of my clients decided to take his grandchildren to Disney World for a week. He knew it would be an expensive trip, but he determined that the quality time he'd have with his grandchildren would be worth the cost. He told me that he'd budgeted about $7,000 for the airfare, hotel, park entrance passes, meals, and other expenses. Unfortunately, the client's cost estimate was not vetted carefully. In fact, it was just an off-the-cuff guess of the cost. You know what happened? The client's budgeted cost ballooned to $15,000 by the time the trip was over. Clearly, a significant underestimation!

The Cost of Freedom on Land and in the Sea and Air

Thinking about a life of freedom on the road, in the water, or in the air is easy and perhaps inspiring. But before you leap, here are some typical costs to consider:

Sailboats and Motorboats: fuel cost, taxes, insurance, dockage fees, maintenance, off-season storage, safety equipment, outfitting the galley and living areas.

Motorcycles: maintenance, gas, insurance, registration and taxes, safety gear, accessories.

Recreational Vehicles: insurance, maintenance, storage fees, camping fees, gas, maintaining a permanent home if you don't live full time in the RV.

Airplanes: insurance, taxes, hangar or tie-down fees, maintenance and expensive regular engine overhauls, required annual inspections, fuel and oil.

month-long tour of Spain's best wineries would not be considered equitable choices.

Budgeting

Do not make creating a budget a rigid and unpleasant chore that causes conflict. After all, you might exceed your budget one year and spend less the next. And as long as your expenses don't exceed any reasonable percentage of your long-term spending assumptions, don't worry about it. Remember, the point of a budget is not to restrain your enjoyment of life or to create conflict, but to liberate you from long-term financial worry.

It's not unusual to imagine taking to the sea or the road or even the air when we retire, and for most people this retirement passion represents only a moderate and manageable expense.

However, sometimes we decide that retirement is the time to upgrade an interest in a lifelong hobby. Perhaps it's a dream to sail to a distant island or country. Or maybe all the adventure that's required is sailing or motoring up and down the East Coast. But no matter the scale or mode of travel—motorcycles, airplanes, or recreational vehicles—it's essential that you carefully calculate the actual cost before you include it in your budget.

I recently went through this calculation with a client who assumed he had the resources to afford a moderately priced motorboat (not a yacht by any measure). First, we calculated the general maintenance for the boat at 10 percent of its value per year, so immediately we added a $25,000 expense line to his boating budget. Then, we added in yearly insurance cost of $4,000 and annual docking fees of $11,000. Next, we thought about how the boat would be used and estimated that just buying fuel would cost at least $10,000 a year. Finally, we added in $4,000 per year for entertaining and other miscellaneous expenses such as keeping the boat's refrigerator well-stocked for visiting friends and relatives. The client also enjoyed fishing, which added a one-time expense of $6,000 to buy appropriate fishing equipment. The total estimate of yearly expenses was at least $55,000, not including the purchase of the boat. After going through the estimation process, the client smartly downsized his boating aspirations.

Smart Consumerism

One of the great advantages of retiring from a job or career you've had for 30 or 40 years is that you now have time to take advantage of your open schedule to be a really smart consumer. That means actively seeking opportunities to reduce the cost of living so you'll have more cash left to do the things you want. Here are some key potential savings to explore when traveling.

▶ **Plan Trips to Europe in September and October.** The weather is beautiful, the streets and roads are less crowded, and the cost difference between high and low seasons is significant. I took my daughter on a short cruise and saved nearly 50 percent by simply moving up our travel by one week.

▶ **Consider Last-Minute Deals.** Check out the many last-minute deal resources on the web, and take advantage of cruise and travel packages offered to those who can travel on short notice. You can expect a savings from 50 to 70 percent off the regular price for these trips. I had a client who paid $3,000 for a two-week European tour that normally was priced at $10,000.

▶ **Don't Pay Full Price for a 4-Star Meal.** A meal at the best restaurant in town is certainly a fine experience, but you can often have lunch at least 40 percent

From Our Practice...
Every Day is a Saturday

A few years ago, I was having a conversation with a friend who was in his late 60s. Although he was still working, his life seemed so busy that I asked him if he used an activities coordinator to keep it all straight. My friend chuckled. "You know, Roy," he said, "most people think life will slow down after they retire, but it's not true. In fact, just the opposite happens. When you retire, every day is a Saturday."

I can't think of a better way to explain what happens to most people who've managed to hold on to enough assets to retire and are fortunate enough to have reasonably good health. Retirement means you are free to focus on your own interests instead of those dictated by your job, business, or family—not that these are forced priorities by any means.

Retirement just might make it possible for you to catch up on this year's five best picture nominees in a single week before Oscar awards are presented. Or you might decide to throw a big dinner party every month. You can also travel when and where you want (assuming it's within your budget) including as many trips as you wish to see grandchildren or to fulfill long-delayed promises to visit friends in far-flung, but interesting, locations.

Of course, all of this activity requires resources from your fixed pool of assets. I can guarantee that no matter the amount budgeted for such entertainment and travel expenses (not to mention all of the other expenses in a retirement budget) your actual monthly cost will outstrip the amount you estimated by a factor of at least two, and more likely three.

It's a lesson most of my clients quickly learn when we work on their budget. For example, a conservative initial estimate by a recent client of $3,500 per month quickly grew to $6,000 and continued to rise to $10,000 as we worked through the budget. Of course, the client was surprised by his lifestyle costs, and if you're reading this book, you already know how I responded. "Yes, it's true what they say. When you're retired, every day is Saturday."

off dinner prices. A friend of mine with an intense interest in food once made lunch reservations at a world-class restaurant in Barcelona when he learned that the typical cost for two during dinner hours was $1,500. Although he could have afforded the meal, he refused to pay that much. He told me his lunch was fabulous and that he enjoyed it even more because he paid a fraction of the suggested cost of an evening meal.

▶ **Use Credit Card Points for Airfare and Lodging.** One of the easiest ways to cut the cost of travel is to use credit cards that allow you to build points that can be traded in for air travel or lodging. You'll be surprised how quickly the miles accumulate. Many credit cards even offer incentive bonus points for joining. Of course, you have to pay the credit card charges off each month to avoid any additional fees. But traveling for free is a great deal that means you'll have more cash to fund your other retirement goals. Some airline credit card perks even include a yearly free companion ticket for one or more family members as part of your member fees.

▶ **Join Home Exchange Networks and Consider Airbnb Lodging Alternatives.** If you think you'd like to spend extended time in another country or region, consider home swap programs such as HomeExchange.com. Other lodging programs such as VRBO (Vacation Rental By Owners) will save you significant amounts of money when you rent the homes of network members for rates far less than any hotel can offer.

A more recent option is Airbnb, which is an online service that connects travelers with airbnb.com members who have extra rooms in their homes to rent out. Once you are approved by the service and the homeowner members, you can take a virtual tour of the available space and then work out the details of your stay. The accommodations (in the most traveled cities around the world) are often better and more conveniently located than the best hotels and cheaper by at least half or more than a similar hotel. Clearly, this isn't an option for everyone, but if you enjoy meeting new people or speak another language and you want to have a more authentic experience, Airbnb just might be for you.

I am advocating these and other money saving approaches because being frugal liberates you and expands your choices in retirement. However, too much focus on saving money curbs your enjoyment of life. The trick is to find an affordable spending balance that lets you do the things that make you happy while still adding fulfillment to your life. After all, as someone once said, there's no advantage to being the richest guy in the morgue.

Healthcare and Long-Term Care

Clearly, one of the most under-estimated aspects of budgeting is paying for the soaring cost of healthcare, particularly the cost of long-term care. As you'll learn in Chapter 6, the cost of nursing home and assisted-living care can be devastating to your retirement saving accounts – with average costs between $3,292 and $6,235 per month. And those are average costs. If you live in an expensive Northeastern city or in desirable locations in California such as Los Angeles and San Francisco, you're likely to pay double these average amounts or more![6]

I also noted in the last chapter that the still untested Affordable Care Act was just rolling out to individual consumers as this book was going to press. I certainly hope the full intention behind the law—affordable healthcare for all Americans—is realized. However, in the meantime I suggest setting aside as much money as possible to pay for potential healthcare expenses, just in case.

Realistic Budgeting

The budget document included in the appendix of this book can also be found on the associated website, OnlyRetireOnce.com. Take a look at the budget and the line items included. You're not likely to know many of the specific figures you'll need to complete the document off the top of your head. After all, most people don't bother to track expenses except in a general way. That is, they know how much they spend on their mortgage, car payments, and other liabilities. Living expenses such as cell phone and cable/wireless connections, home utilities, groceries, and fuel costs are much harder to quantify. That's okay. There's a lot more to think about before you actually dig into the details. For now, just note some of the major listings and keep them in mind as you continue reading.

What's Next and Wrap Up

Chapter 4 will reveal some key strategies to ensure a reliable cash flow to meet the expenses of the budget you eventually create. I'll also give you some pointers on how to determine the right amount of cash reserves for your unique financial situation.

Here's a recap of the key information presented in this chapter:

▶ A well thought out budget means liberation, not limitation. It's an empowering document you will use to guide the rest of your life.

▶ Respect the power of inflation to reduce the value of your portfolio.

▶ Yes, you will spend more than you can imagine. Plan accordingly.

▶ Set aside cash to help you recover from both major and minor disasters in your home.

▶ Carefully plan your lifestyle and be a smart consumer.

Use Smart Asset Management to Ensure Steady Cash Flow

In This Chapter

▶ Minimize Portfolio Risk

▶ Avoid Too Much Leverage

▶ Manage Allocations and Withdrawals

▶ Determine Optimal Cash Reserve

So you've done it. You've officially retired! You feel good about your strong, diversified portfolio and its ability to sustain the lifestyle you've planned. You've created a sustainable budget that takes into account every potential drain on your cash flow including a few you still insist will never happen. Now, all you have to do is sit back and relax, right? No worries, just chill and let the money roll in.

Well, maybe . . . but my experience says that's not a good assumption. Yes, it's true some people do have portfolios large enough to weather any substantial market correction or other reductions in their expected returns. But for most investors, retirement is likely to mean *more* retirement budget scrutiny not *less*.

Deadly Mistake #4

Inconsistent Income

This chapter offers some key strategies that will keep you on track to maintain a reliable cash flow. Some asset-management strategies, such as the need to minimize your investment risk, are easy to understand, while other strategies are more nuanced and are intended to help you minimize your tax burden while extending the life of your investment portfolio.

You'll also find tips and strategies to determine an optimal amount of cash reserves you'll need in retirement. As noted in the previous chapter, this cash reserve amount can vary from six months of expenses to as much as two years.

Financial Risk-taking Before Retirement

The amount of risk most of us are willing to take—whether it's taking up the sport of skydiving, doing freestyle rock climbing, participating in competitive motorcycle racing, or just driving too fast on the freeway—is directly proportional to the potential consequences if something goes wrong. So that means when we're not weighed down with family and career commitments it's easy to throw caution to the wind and dance right on the edge of financial disaster to get the highest returns.

Of course, most of us eventually do sign up for the real life of family commitments, which means we do everything possible to *avoid* excessive financial risk. Unfortunately, many middle-aged (and older) Americans continue to approach financial risk, particularly leveraged debt in the form of variable rate loans, like an unencumbered 25-year-old.

As a historical reminder, in 2003, adjustable rate mortgage (ARM) loans accounted for only about 0.5 percent of all mortgages written that year. By 2006, the overall percentage of ARM loans accounted for more than 12 percent of all loans nationwide. Hot housing bubble markets at the time, such as those in California and Florida, reported that 40 percent of all loans were ARMs.[1] Of course, we all know what happened two years later when the house of cards crashed resulting in the 2008 mortgage crisis that nearly tanked the economy.

Yes, it is a great deal to get a 2.5 or 3.0 percent initial rate loan. The savings are appealing in the short term. But when these rates rise—as they certainly will at some point—many individuals and businesses end up struggling to make the higher monthly payments.

That's why I tell my clients, including those approaching their retirement years, to avoid these loans and opt instead for reliable fixed-interest rates even if the interest rates are higher. However, in some cases, with a disciplined, younger investor these loans do have a useful purpose, especially if the investor intends to sell a property before mortgage rates adjust up. Still, in general, ARMs are risky bets that should be avoided.

Asset Risk Management

How much financial risk you're willing to tolerate decreases as you age. So, if you're within five years of retirement your appetite for risk is less than if retirement is 30 years away. That's why I advise some of my clients to take their retirement portfolio on a test drive about five years prior to their actual retirement date. Clearly, this works best for clients who survived the last couple of market corrections financially intact and don't need to take advantage of every possible strategy to catch up.

In any case, the idea is to design a portfolio that doesn't take any unnecessary risk. Once the plan is implemented, we monitor the portfolio and rebalance it tactically to ensure the asset mix does in fact produce the income we've projected.

The Vagaries of Investing

We all know that investing is a game of risk and that, in general, greater risks

---

How Bond Prices Affect Interest Rates

Bonds are debt investments used by companies, cities, states, and governments to finance projects or other needed activities.

Investors loan money to these entities by issuing a bond for a certain amount of time at a fixed or locked-in rate. These investments are often called fixed-income securities because a certain level of return is fixed.

An inverse relationship exists between bond prices and interest rates. This means that if interest rates rise, bond prices fall. If interest rates fall, bond prices rise. [2]

means greater returns and less risk means less returns. The job of a financial advisor is to chart an investment course that provides a reasonable rate of return over time so that your life and retirement goals are achieved. Unfortunately, this steady and slow philosophy is sometimes ignored by the larger investment community and the lure of easy money (and lots of it) trumps common sense. And that's when a proverbial market crash occurs. Here are some recent examples of such overheated investment markets:

▶ On October 19, 1987, stock markets around the world crashed on a day known as Black Monday. The Dow Jones fell 22.6 percent from 2,246 to 1,734. Then, in 1989 a booming real estate and housing market crashed, and millions of individuals and businesses were left holding properties worth much less than the purchase price.[3]

▶ The dot-com bubble began inflating around 1997 and was spurred on by out-of-control venture capitalists eager to fund almost any back-of-the-envelope business plan presented by the proliferation of young, energetic internet entrepreneurs. NASDAQ technology stocks peaked at 5,408 on March 10, 2000, a level that was more than double its value just the year before.

▶ Then, the high-tech bubble began to deflate, and tech investments lost more than $5 trillion of value between 2000 and 2002. While some survivors of the era (including Amazon.com) were good long-term bets, other exuberant but misguided decisions such as the America Online and Time Warner merger were a debacle of historic proportions. In fact, the AOL and Time Warner merger is generally regarded as the worst merger in U.S. history.[4]

▶ Then there's the all too familiar 2008 Great Recession. This market correction resulted in a 50 percent drop in market value from its October 9, 2007 high when the Dow Jones reached a level of 14,164. Only the Great Depression of 1929 produced a greater drop when it lost 80 percent of its market value nearly overnight.[5]

I've worked with and advised some casualties of these recent economic downturns, and it's sad to see the effect. During the last market correction, one couple came to me for advice because their portfolio had lost more than 60 percent of its value. They had retired early and decided to keep riding the rising stock market wave rather than diversify their investments toward safer, less volatile investments. Unfortunately, the only option I could offer them was the advice to go back to work.

It seems like such a simple bit of financial savvy, to not put all your investments in the proverbial single basket, but it continues to be a frequent investing mistake. Don't bet on a single company, sector, or country. Instead, create a plan that will meet your retirement goals by providing a reasonable return for a reasonable amount of risk.

The Power of Compound Interest

You probably know the story of how the Native Americans (known as the Lenape) sold the island now called Manhattan in 1626 for a few beads and other worthless trinkets. This famous story is true up to a point. The Lenape did in fact trade the Big Apple for trinkets, but apparently they got a whole trunk load of trinkets in the trade and not just a handful as the story implies. What's not true about this story is that the trinkets offered by Dutch dealmaker Peter Minuit were worthless. In fact, the Lenape's treasure

When To Use a Financial Planner

Most people don't need financial help early in their careers because they are still just building an asset base. But as your assets build value over time so does the risk of making an investment mistake that undermines your long-term financial security. For most people, the best age range for seeking professional advice is somewhere between the ages of 45 and 50 because that's when most careers begin to pay the highest financial rewards.

In the meantime, if your company offers a 401(k) plan, it's a good idea to use the online (and often in-person) advice resources and management tools to monitor and rebalance your investment mix to suit current market conditions. If you are not comfortable making these investment decisions with available resources, then by all means, get some professional advice. After all, it's your money and financial future on the line.

Russia: A Hot Investment that Crashed

In the late 1990s, investing in the emerging market-based economy of Russia was hot. Then between January and August of 1998, the boom went bust and the Russian stock market lost nearly 80% of its value. Even when the market rebounded by 100% the following year, any investment made during the crash still left investors down by 60 percent, Worse, these investors would need a 400 percent return just to get even with the original value.[8]

was worth about 60 Netherland guilders (or $24) at the time.[6]

In today's economy, $24 is hardly enough to buy two entrees at the Times Square Olive Garden. However, had the Indians invested even a portion of the trinkets' cash value in a standard bank savings account that paid an annual interest rate of 5 percent and let it build compound interest over the next 387 years, the Lenape descendants would be worth about $6.07 billion today.[7]

Of course, you don't have 400 years to reap the benefits of compound interest savings. Still, the story is a good illustration of what our parents and grandparents told us about saving just a little every month; it adds up!

Financial Risk-taking After Retirement

As I pointed out at the beginning of this chapter, retirement means more focus on finance and budgets, not less because a fixed budget's cash flow depends on the steady performance of the invested assets.

Yet I frequently talk to investors attending one of my retirement-planning workshops who have never rebalanced their employer-provided 401(k) despite our volatile economy. I've even talked with former executives with millions of dollars in investments who don't pay attention to the overall performance of their portfolio.

The fact is, no one can afford to risk the long-term value in their retirement portfolio due to negligence. Nor can you make planning decisions based on a hot tip from a friend or former colleague or because a famous investing guru said a particular company or stock was a good bet. Once you're retired, every investing decision is critical and so finding a trusted advisor is absolutely essential.

Not that professional financial advice is always right, but given a choice between the subjective advice of a friend and any other random advice you might receive, professional retirement-planning advice offered by someone who understands your long-term goals and dreams is a much better option.

Asset Allocations and Withdrawals

Financial planners often use the terms *retirement* and *nonretirement* accounts. You may already understand the meaning, but I'll briefly explain these terms.

A *retirement* asset is any investment asset—including annuities—held in a tax-deferred account such as an individual retirement account (IRA) or 401(k). These assets also include any taxable portion of survivor benefits from a traditional defined employer pension plan or a Roth IRA. (Note: Taxes are paid up front on a Roth IRA so this bends the definition a bit because no taxes are paid when funds are withdrawn.) The idea behind these investments is that the funds grow over the years as a tax-deferred asset and taxes are paid at your ordinary income rate when withdrawn.

Nonretirement assets are assets you, your spouse, or a trust owns. It also includes investments such as stocks, bonds, and mutual funds. Unlike retirement assets such as a 401(k), the amount of money you can invest in these accounts is not limited and taxes paid on gains are levied at a much lower rate

Five-Star Tip: Be Careful When Loaning Money

You've probably heard all of your life that lending money to a friend can be a gateway to a whole list of unintended consequences, not the least of which is the possibility that your act of friendship or kindness is never repaid.

So, I'll just say it again: think carefully about loaning money to your friends or relatives! And if you do decide to be generous, here are two tips—one obvious and one for prudence's sake. **One:** if you think you'll need the money in the future and can't really afford to lose it, curb your philanthropic urges. **Two:** make sure you run a credit check on the potential friend or family member debtor.

It's not about the basic moral character of the debtor—although it might indeed be an issue. It's just good business practice, and it's about taking care of yourself and protecting your retirement assets so that the money is there when you need it.

Amount of Market Decline	20% Decline	40% Decline	60% Decline	80% Decline
Starting Asset Value	$10,000	$10,000	$10,000	$10,000
Amount of Asset Decline	$2,000	$4,000	$6,000	$8,000
New Asset Value	$8,000	$6,000	$4,000	$2,000
Return Percentage Needed to Reclaim Original Value	25%	67%	150%	400%

Figure 4.1. Assets in a Declining Market

(15% to 23.8% plus any applicable state and local taxes) when withdrawn. Remember, depending on your income, withdrawals from traditional retirement accounts can take as much as a 39 percent tax bite.

Retirement and Nonretirement Asset Strategies

Determining how and when you tap into retirement and nonretirement accounts is a delicate balancing act that is usually detailed in a comprehensive retirement income plan. Later in this book, I'll offer key tax savings and social security income considerations, but for now, here are some basic strategies to keep in mind.

First, you should know that financial and investment professionals assign different levels of risk to each of your investment accounts depending on factors such as your age, retirement goals, and when you plan to begin living exclusively on retirement assets. So, a 60-year-old able to delay drawing on Social Security funds until the maximum benefits age is reached at age 70 while also continuing to work until age 66 or 67 would be able to tolerate more asset risk than someone who needs to access their Social Security assets at age 62 or 65.

The exact ratio of retirement and non-retirement assets you ultimately rely upon depends on your overall goals and objectives coupled with smart strategies that minimize the taxes you pay. For example, a plan that relies heavily on non-retirement assets such as stock dividends to provide 25 percent of your monthly cash flow (in addition to Social Security benefits and pension payments) is not very risky. For someone in their 50s or 60s who is in a low tax bracket now, an advisor might suggest that a way to reduce the risk of paying high taxes in the future would be to reduce non-retirement withdrawals while increasing the amount drawn from retirement assets such as your IRA or 401(k). By taking some of the money to fund retirement before 70-1/2 from the IRA or 401(k) before it is required, you reduce the mandatory 70-1/2 distribution requirement, and, therefore your projected future tax liability. However, if you're under 59-1/2, you'll need to use rule 72 (t) to avoid the 10 percent early withdrawal penalty.

Typically, I put a five-year plan together with my clients that identifies the specific income sources they'll use to fund the objectives we've established. In most cases, this income plan is a carefully orchestrated mix of income streams from the client's retirement and nonretirement assets along with Social Security and the client's defined pension income. In addition to this income plan, we look at specific tax strategies that will benefit both the client's income stream and the achievement of their retirement goals. Some of these specific tax strategies are explained in detail later in the book.

Assets in Volatile Markets

The best way to demonstrate why having an asset management strategy is so critical to successful retirement is with a graphic illustration showing how wide swings in the stock market affect nonretirement assets. Figure 4.1 illustrates how long it takes to recover from a steep market decline. For example, if your assets lost 20 percent of value during one of these swings, then you'd need a 25 percent positive gain just to recapture the value of the original portfolio. A 50 percent loss would require a gain of 100 percent, and a devastating 80 percent loss would require a compensating 400 percent gain in value to retain the original value.

Historical CD Rates

Year	Percent	Year	Percent	Year	Percent	Year	Percent
1965	4.43	1979	11.44	1993	3.28	2007	5.23
1966	5.63	1980	12.99	1994	4.96	2008	3.14
1967	5.21	1981	15.77	1995	5.98	2009	0.88
1968	6.00	1982	12.57	1996	5.47	2010	0.44
1969	7.89	1983	9.27	1997	5.72	2011	0.42
1970	7.66	1984	10.68	1998	5.44	2012	0.44
1971	5.22	1985	8.25	1999	5.46		
1972	5.02	1986	6.51	2000	6.58		
1973	8.31	1987	7.00	2001	3.64		
1974	9.98	1988	7.90	2002	1.81		

Figure 4.2.

The reason for the disparity between the market value loss and the compensating marketplace gain is because these losses are effectively liquidating part of a portfolio's value and earnings potential.

So, if the value of your $10,000 portfolio fell 20 percent to $8,000, you would need to earn 25 percent or $2,000 on the lower $8,000 value to get back to the original $10,000 market value. This swing in value directly affects your retirement budget's cash flow. For example, if you were depending on a 5 percent yearly return on this original $10,000 investment ($500) and the market value suddenly fell by 50 percent, then the same asset (now worth $5,000) would need to generate a 10 percent return to continue providing the same $500 yearly contribution—not a very likely scenario.

If you add to this disaster scenario the effect of an average 4 percent inflation rate, then it's easy to see why you'd soon run out of money in retirement. It's sad, really, how many times I see this portfolio value-loss scenario play out in my practice. Yes, sometimes a few people are lucky and make big gains by pursuing risky, high-yield investment strategies. That's why for most investors slow and steady ultimately wins the race of life.

The Effect of Inflation on Asset Allocation

Inflation is the silent killer of retirement asset value so it's essential to appreciate the potential financial risk it poses before and after retirement.

One of the best illustrations of this value struggle is a typical certificate of deposit account (CD). Millions of Americans still have their entire retirement savings in CDs even when the average interest rate on a five-year CD is about 1.5 percent. Current six-month returns on CDs are even less.[9] Clearly, with inflation averaging 4 percent, the buying power of each dollar in these accounts loses value every year. It's pretty difficult to construct a secure retirement scenario when retirement assets are continuously losing purchasing power.

It's important to note that CDs were once one of the best places to park your money and watch it grow. According to ForecastChart. com, the average return for CDs between 1979 and 1989 exceeded 11 percent with a highpoint of nearly 16 percent reached in 1981. These hefty rates are unlikely to return any time soon, but CDs are still a safe and relatively accessible place to hold emergency cash reserves. CDs are still good places to keep

Example of a Bull Market

Year	Total Annual Return with Dividends for S&P 500
2003	28.68%
2004	10.88%
2005	4.91%
2006	15.79%
2007	5.49%
2008	-37.00%
2009	26.46%
2010	15.06%
2011	2.11%
2012	16.00%
2013	32.39%

Figure 4.3

Example of a Bear Market

Year	Total Annual Return with Dividends for S&P 500
2000	-9.10%
2001	-11.89%
2002	-22.10%
2003	28.68%
2004	10.88%
2005	4.91%
2006	15.79%
2007	5.49%
2008	-37.00%
2009	26.46%
2010	15.06%
2011	2.11%
2012	16.00%

Figure 4.4

cash in anticipation of buying a first or second home or to fund an upcoming wedding for a son or daughter once the date is set. Otherwise leave the money in a cash account.[10]

Your Income Stream

One of the most consistent bits of advice I give my clients is to pay all of the taxes they owe, but not a dime more than necessary. That's not surprising advice, but the fact is many retirees pay more tax than necessary due to the way they take distributions from taxable retirement and nonretirement accounts. Remember a distribution from a 401(k) account is taxed according to your top ordinary income tax bracket rate (up to 39.5%) and qualified dividend income is taxed at the top capital gains rate (either 0, 15, or 20%). So, how and when you take distributions matters a great deal.

For example, it may be a much better strategy to sell appreciated stock and take the cash because the taxes you'll pay are determined by the stock's increase in value over the original purchase price. On a traditional IRA, the entire qualified distribution is taxed at your ordinary income. And if you or your financial advisor is savvy enough, you might save on taxes by cashing shares out on a stock with minimal gains or those investments showing a capital loss and then using the transaction loss to reduce your taxable income and thus your yearly tax bill.

Returns Sequencing

Many of the investment-return scenarios noted in this chapter are about long-term or average rates of return and how these averages affect your financial health after retirement. But actually, the timing of your retirement and the economic conditions at the time you retire can have a huge effect on your long-term financial security. Financial experts call this sequence risk.[11]

What this means in practical terms is that if you retire right after a bull market (market trending up), your chances of achieving your investment goals over the next 30 or so years are much better than if you happen to retire at the top of a bear market (market trending down). (See Figures 4.3 and 4.4 for examples of returns on these markets.)

Here is how this investment scenario assumption might play out on an investment portfolio of $100,000. Let's say you retired January 1st in 2003

What Is an Annuity?

An annuity is a contract between you and a provider (usually an insurance company) that guarantees your investment with the provider is returned to you in guaranteed regular payments at some future date.

These investments usually grow tax-deferred, but are taxed at ordinary tax rates upon withdrawal. Early withdrawal results in tax penalties as well as substantial fines levied by the provider.

A fixed annuity pays the contract owner a specified rate of interest and disburses funds in specified dollar amounts.

An indexed annuity pays returns based on changes in an index, such as the S&P 500, with payments made in specific amounts no matter how the index performs.

A variable annuity is typically tied to mutual fund investments chosen by the contract owner. Payments made vary depending on the performance of the investment choices.[12]

(definitely a bull market) when the annual returns for the S&P were 28.68 percent, the Dow Jones was 28.2 percent, and the NASDAQ was 50.77 percent. Over the next 10 years, your $100,000 investment would be worth $262,822.80, even with the 2008 market crash.

If you had retired on January 1, 2001, with the same $100,000 portfolio during a bear market when the annual returns for the S&P were 11.89 percent, the Dow Jones was 5.50 percent, and the NASDAQ was 20.82 percent, your retirement portfolio would be worth only $117,466.10!

The dramatic performance difference between bull and bear markets demonstrates why optimization of returns is so important, and it's why so many Americans still say they can't afford to retire even with the return of better market conditions. It's very difficult to make up for these losses even with impressive gains. This is especially true when taking distributions income.

Annuities

An annuity is an investment product used primarily to provide a steady cash flow during retirement.   Payments can be structured to pay a fixed amount of cash on a recurring periodic basis (monthly, quarterly) or on a less regular or variable basis, i.e., more cash withdrawals when investment income is down. Depending on the annuity contract terms and conditions, annuities can be paid out to a specified beneficiary or to an estate.

Some financial specialists don't recommend annuities under any circumstance, but I occasionally recommend the investment if doing so satisfies the client's overall investment goals and risk tolerance. For example, an annuity is a good choice for someone interested in a guaranteed income stream who also doesn't mind forgoing higher returns or if we have to take significant risk because a client doesn't have enough now to retire on. Still, I do offer a few investment caveats:

▶ Don't risk all annuity assets in a single company because these companies sometimes have financial difficulties.

▶ Choose the lower fee product if benefits are equal.

▶ Guarantees are only as good as the company backing them.

Not Tax Efficient

From a tax standpoint, annuities, depending on the source of the funds, are not always tax efficient. For example, purchasing an annuity with nonretirement accounts assets may not be the best choice because you'll be changing the taxation of the assets from capital gains to taxation at ordinary income tax rates.

Here are some other cautions about annuities you should consider before investing:

▶ Although annuities ensure a steady cash flow, understand that you are locking up money for the specified contract period.

▶ Make sure you know the guarantees provided and how the payouts are calculated. Some companies calculate returns on a daily average, and that may not be such a good deal for you.

▶ Research the annuity company choices carefully. Some companies have 10-year surrender periods; others offer three years, while others have no surrender period.

What's Next and Wrap Up

Chapter 5 examines key strategies to use when choosing how you receive Social Security payments, the benefits and risks of re-entering the workforce post-retirement, and guidance on a full range of other Social Security challenges including advice for widow(er)s and divorcees.

Here's a recap of the key information presented in this chapter:

▶ The amount of financial risk most of us are willing to take is directly proportional to the potential consequences if something goes wrong, and our proximity to retirement age.

▶ Avoid adjustable rate mortgages even if the rates are substantially lower than fixed rate loans.

▶ The job of your financial advisor is to chart an investment course that provides an acceptable rate of return over time by taking reasonable and appropriate risks.

▶ Be careful when loaning money to friends and relatives. Trust but verify.

▶ Creating a plan for a steady cash flow is a delicate balancing act that requires a comprehensive retirement income plan strategy that carefully examines how and when you tap into retirement and nonretirement accounts.

▶ Parking cash in a CD is an acceptable financial strategy if you anticipate buying a first or second home or will soon fund a special event such as a wedding. Otherwise leave the money in a cash account.

▶ Retiring in a bull market (a market trending up) is much, much better than retiring in a bear market (a market trending down).

▶ Annuities do provide a steady and predictable income stream in retirement, but make sure you understand the tradeoffs.

Don't Leave Social Security Benefits on the Table

In This Chapter

▶ Maximize Social Security Benefits

▶ Choose the Best Time to Retire

▶ Deal with Special Retirement Circumstances

According to a 2012 report by the Social Security Administration's (SSA's) board of trustees, Social Security is fully funded until at least 2033. After that, depending on which set of economic projections used, partial to full funding will continue for the next 30 years.[1] That's good news for anyone retiring in the near term and just another reason to maximize your Social Security benefits as much as possible.

This chapter will help you make the most informed decision about when and how to begin taking Social Security benefits. While it might seem a straightforward decision, the details can be confusing and, if not interpreted correctly, even costly. This chapter will help you avoid these mistakes by offering:

▶ Guidance on choosing *when* and *how* Social Security payments are made

Deadly Mistake #5

Selecting the Wrong Social Security Benefits

▶ Strategies to maximize benefits for both dual- and single-income households

▶ Advice on re-entering the workforce after retirement

▶ Strategies for retiring with children still under age 18

▶ Tips and advice on retiring single, widowed, or divorced.

Boomer Retirement Considerations

It's hard to imagine that 10,000 American baby boomers on average reach retirement age each day—a prospect that is even harder to fathom if you are one of these boomers surprised about how quickly you arrived at this work-exit queue.[2] That sense of wonder aside, it's clear why so many in this generation of retirees have such grave concerns about their financial future. As I pointed out in the last chapter, the long-term viability of your asset and investment portfolio has a great deal to do with when you retire and the state of the economy at the time you retire. So if you retire during a rising market tide, your portfolio will benefit and your long-term financial prospects will likely be good. If the market tide is receding when you retire, your portfolio of investments will likely suffer and you'll need to rely more on Social Security benefits to meet cash flow needs.

Inflation and Your Bottom Line

Inflation really is the silent killer of retirement assets. Over time inflation destroys the spending power of every dollar you've saved. Congress addressed this economic reality for retirees in 1972 by enacting a Cost of Living Adjustment (COLA) provision to the existing Social Security law. COLA automatically adjusts retiree benefits in response to the rate of inflation as measured by the Consumer Price Index for

Urban Wage Earners and Clerical Workers (CPI-W), which is an economic calculation prepared by the Bureau of Labor Statistics. Note that the actual COLA increases over the years have varied between 0 and 14.3 percent due to a complex formulation that I won't detail here. (See Figure 5.1.) As a practical matter, some years the COLA is above the average yearly inflation rate of 4 percent and some years the COLA is less. Here is what Social Security has to say about COLA increases:

"For purposes of determining the COLA, the average CPI-W for the third calendar quarter of the last year a COLA was determined is compared to the average CPI-W for the third calendar quarter of the current year. The resulting percentage increase, if any, represents the percentage that will be used to increase Social Security benefits beginning for December

A Very Brief History of Social Security

President Franklin Roosevelt signed the Social Security Act into law on August 14, 1935, but it took five years to set up the program, collect the taxes, and send out the initial lump-sum payment to the first wave of American retirees in January of 1940.[3]

For millions of Americans who had been financially ruined by the post–Great Depression economy that began in 1929, this payment was no doubt a Godsend. And despite recognizable controversies at the time about starting a new, expensive government program, it was affordable because about 45 working Americans supported a single retiree. Today, that supporting ratio is two workers for every one retiree—clearly, not a sustainable model.

As I pointed out earlier in this book, the supporting math is further complicated by the fact that a relatively few retirees lived more than 10 years past their retirement date. Today, 80-year-old retirees scale mountains, skydive, and sometimes even start third careers.

Clearly, the system can't afford to pay Social Security benefits to every living American with a steady work history. My own prediction is that the solution may require the creation of a needs-based system; that is, if you need the assistance it will be available.

of the current year. SSI benefits increase by the same percentage the following month (January). If the increase in the CPI-W is at least one-tenth of one percent (0.1 percent), there will be a COLA. However, if the CPI-W increases by less than 0.05 percent, or if the CPI-W decreases, there will not be a COLA."[4]

Automatic Cost-of-Living Adjustments	
July 1975 – 8.0%	Jan. 1996 – 2.6%
July 1976 – 6.4%	Jan. 1997 – 2.9%
July 1977 – 5.9%	Jan. 1998 – 2.1%
July 1978 – 6.5%	Jan. 1999 – 1.3%
July 1979 – 9.9%	Jan. 2000 – 2.5%[1]
July 1980 – 14.3%	Jan. 2001 – 3.5%
July 1981 – 11.2%	Jan. 2002 – 2.6%
July 1982 – 7.4%	Jan. 2003 – 1.4%
Jan. 1984 – 3.5%	Jan. 2004 – 2.1%
Jan. 1985 – 3.5%	Jan. 2005 – 2.7%
Jan. 1986 – 3.1%	Jan. 2006 – 4.1%
Jan. 1987 – 1.3%	Jan. 2007 – 3.3%
Jan. 1988 – 4.2%	Jan. 2008 – 2.3%
Jan. 1989 – 4.0%	Jan. 2009 – 5.8%
Jan. 1990 – 4.7%	Jan. 2010 – 0%
Jan. 1991 – 5.4%	Jan. 2011 – 0%
Jan. 1992 – 3.7%	Jan. 2012 – 3.6%
Jan. 1993 – 3.0%	Jan. 2013 – 1.7%
Jan. 1994 – 2.6%	Jan. 2014 – 1.3%
Jan. 1995 – 2.8%	

[1] The COLA for Dec. 1999 was originally determined as 2.4 percent based on CPIs published by the Bureau of Labor Statistics. Pursuant to Public Law 106-554, however, this COLA is effectively now 2.5 percent.

Figure 5.1

COLA and Your Bottom Line

If you're interested in the arcane technical details behind these adjustments, visit the SSA website (www.ssa.com). You'll find an excruciating level of detail. However, as a practical matter, the most important consideration for most of us is how these Social Security benefit adjustments are incorporated into our comprehensive retirement strategy.

SSA always announces the COLA benefit increase a few months before the end of the previous year. That's important information if you're planning to retire during the coming year because the announced COLA affects the base rate for your lifetime monthly benefit. If the COLA is low, it might be worth delaying retirement until the next year when the COLA rate might adjust higher.

In 2010 and 2011, the COLA was 0 percent because inflation was low due to the lingering effect of the financial crisis. Then, in 2012 the COLA was pegged at 3.6 percent due to a slight rise in the inflation rate that year. In 2013, the COLA was 1.7 percent, and the COLA forecast for 2014 was 1.3 percent.[5]

Now, imagine that you had planned to retire in 2010 or 2011 and, based on that year's COLA, your monthly benefit was set at $2,100 per month. In 20 years (without subsequent COLA increases added in) your SSA payments would amount to $504,000. But what if you decided to delay retirement for one or two years and instead retired in 2012 when the COLA was 3.6 percent?

Making this choice would mean that instead of getting $2,100 per month, your base benefit would be set at $2,176. Over a 20-year period that would translate into an additional $18,240 benefit increase. Note that this amount assumes an additional 8 percent benefit plus COLA. If the individual was still working and earned a higher income than in previous years, the benefit would be even more. Still, the important point to remember here is that COLA benefits only matter when you retire. The essential strategy here is that by waiting to begin receiving benefits at age 70 you establish the base benefit amount that the SSA uses to compound all future COLA benefits.

SSA Eligibility Guidelines

A visit to the Social Security website (www.ssa.gov) is a good starting point to understand your potential benefits. Here's the official eligibility chart published on the website.[6]

Year of Birth	Full Retirement Age
1937 or earlier	65
1938	65 and 2 months
1939	65 and 4 months
1940	65 and 6 months
1941	65 and 8 months
1942	65 and 10 months
1943-54	66
1955	66 and 2 months
1956	66 and 4 months
1957	66 and 6 months
1958	66 and 8 months
1959	66 and 10 months
1960 and later	67

Note: If you quality for benefits as a Survivor, your full retirement age may be different. • If you were born on Jan. 1st of nay hear, you shoud refer to the previous year. Source: Social Security Administration

Figure 5.2

Retirement Factors

Clearly, COLA is an important factor in your retirement decision, but these adjustments are not the whole picture. You'll also need to consider factors such as your current health, your family's history of longevity, the value of retirement and nonretirement account investments, your marital status and relative earnings as compared to your spouse's, and your own gut sense that the time is right to retire.

Balancing all of these factors is difficult if not impossible to do alone. That's why it's critical to examine all of the options with a retirement, tax, or other financial expert. While this book certainly provides a great deal of important information, the safest and best option is to find an expert you trust and then rely on their advice and guidance

Full or Normal Retirement Age

Full retirement age is determined by your birth year and ranges from 65 to 67 years old. While it is possible to retire at 62, you will lose as much as 30% of your normal retirement monthly benefit by claiming early.

If you delay retirement, you'll get an 8% credit for each year you delay until age 70. That means a 64% difference between the ages of 62 and 70 for someone with a normal retirement age of 66.

So, for example, if your full retirement age benefit at 66 was $2,000 per month waiting just four years would mean an increase in monthly benefits to $2,640.

as well as your own research. It's also good to do a little networking and ask friends or colleagues who they would recommend. Often a personal recommendation is the best recommendation.

Retirement-Age Considerations

Eligible Social Security beneficiaries can begin receiving retirement benefits any time between the ages of 62 and 70. (Note: Widows can begin receiving benefits at age 60.) However, it's typically best to delay claiming benefits until you reach your full retirement age (FRA) as determined by your birth year. (See Figure 5.2.)

For example, a baby boomer born between 1943 and 1954 can begin collecting full retirement benefits beginning at age 66 (or between 2009 and 2020). If you were born in 1960 or later, the FRA is 67 (or beginning in 2026).

Substantial reductions are attached to taking Social Security benefits before FRA, and the percentage decreases levied also vary according to birth year. For example, if you reached age 62 in 2013 (a 1951 birthdate) and applied for benefits, your full retirement benefit would be cut by 25 percent. If you were born after 1959 and plan to retire at age 62 your full retirement benefit will be cut by 30 percent.

Clearly, delaying retirement until at least FRA is a good idea if possible, but the fact is that not everyone can afford to wait that long. Sometimes circumstances such as a late-career job loss or major health crisis gives us no choice. In these dire situations, if the choice is between accumulating long-term debt and collecting a Social Security benefit early, it is almost always the better choice to avoid the debt.

But barring any financial or health disasters, here are some key benefit strategies to consider.

Living in Dual-Income Households

Dual-income households do have a few more strategy options than single-income households. As noted, the longer an individual retiree delays collecting benefits, the greater the benefit payment. The maximizing strategy is called file-and-suspend. Here's an example:

If one spouse in a married couple files for their own benefit, then the other can claim a spousal benefit up to half

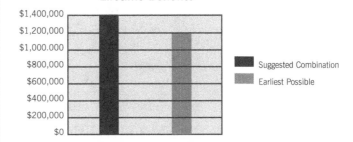

Strategy Comparison
The expected lifetime family benefit using the **suggested** strategy is $1,385,517
The expected lifetime family benefit for the **earliest** available combination is $1,206,654

Lifetime Benefits

Suggested Combination
Earliest Possible

Graph represents present value of Lifetime Family Benefits.
The preceeding chart and comparisons assume that John dies at age 90 years and Jane dies at age 90 years.

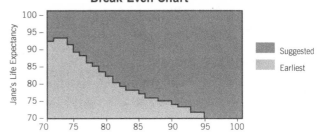

Break Even Chart

Suggested
Earliest

Graph illustrates which of the outlined strategies provide the best outcome at any given set of whole year death age combinations. Break Even points occur at combinations where the strategy offering the best outcome changes. The suggested strategy was determined by assuming John dies at 90 years and Jane dies at 90 years.

Figure 5.3

of the primary benefit amount of the other spouse, letting their own benefit increase 8 percent yearly until age 70 before they switch to the higher benefit. Plus, the surviving spouse receives the greater of the two benefits.

This is a good strategy for adding extra income while letting one benefit grow at a guaranteed increase of 8 percent. In the right circumstance, a couple could use this strategy until they both reached the maximum benefit age of 70. Here's a narrative illustration of this spousal benefit strategy:

Fred is 66 years and five months, and Marti has just turned 66 years old. Fred files a standard application to begin collecting retirement benefits; his FRA benefit is $2,566.

Fred immediately requests that his benefit be suspended, which will allow him to earn delayed retirement credits during the time the benefit is suspended. When Fred turns 70, he requests that his benefit be paid with a monthly benefit of $3,470.

Marti files a restricted application for only the spousal benefit based on Fred's earnings record so her spousal benefit would be about $1,283. Doing so allows Marti to continue to earn delayed retirement credits on her own benefit so that when Marti reaches age 70 she files for her own benefit based on her own earning record, which would be $3,654 per month. If Fred and Marti followed this strategy, they could expect to collect $1,385,517 over the course of their expected lifetimes. (See Figure 5.3.)

Living in Single-Income Households

Single individuals also have some viable options to maximize their Social Security benefits. The first is to simply delay filing for Social Security benefits for as long as possible. If you can delay until age 70, then the effect on cash flow is significant. Think of this delaying strategy as earning a guaranteed 8 percent return on an investment. Another strategy is to use state and federal tax laws to minimize taxes and maximize your income stream in retirement.

For example, 15 percent of an individual's Social Security payment is federal tax-free. So if you had to choose between taking Social Security benefits at age 62 and withdrawing funds from your IRA retirement account to meet cash flow needs, the best choice would be to start receiving your benefits. That's because if you take Social Security benefits you are paying ordinary income tax on 15 percent of the benefit rather than ordinary income tax on the full amount of your IRA withdrawal.

Someone with considerable assets in a retirement account can delay paying taxes on a portion of the withdrawals from retirement and nonretirement accounts by receiving that extra income filing for benefits at age 62. Over the long-term, this tax strategy could add up to significant savings.

Claiming Ages for Widows and Percentage of Survivor Benefit	
Claiming Age	% of Survivor Benefit
60	71.50
61	76.25
62	81.00
63	85.75
64	90.40
65	95.25
66	100.00

Figure 5.4

Tax laws are different in each state (some states have no state income tax and others have high income tax) so the effectiveness of this strategy also depends on these differing tax laws.

Living as Divorcees

Divorced individuals who are 62 years or older, unmarried, and not entitled to a higher Social Security benefit on their own record can receive benefits as a divorced spouse on a former spouse's Social Security record if they were married for at least 10 years and if the former spouse is at least 62 years old.

Under this scenario, the benefits paid would be exactly the same as for a married couple. The ex-spouse could claim spousal benefits at age 66 and would be eligible for a survivor benefit at age 60. And the benefit for a current wife is not affected by a divorcee's spouse.

Social Security does not pay benefits if the divorced spouse remarries someone other than the former spouse, unless the remarriage ends (whether by death, divorce, or annulment) or the marriage is to a person entitled to certain types of Social Security auxiliary or survivor's benefits.

Even when a former spouse dies, it is possible to claim benefits as the surviving divorced spouse if the surviving ex-spouse is unmarried, at least 60 years old and was married to the former spouse for at least 10 years.

Living as Widows and Widowers

Life expectancy has increased dramatically, and as I pointed out in the first pages of this book, a long life is a basic assumption for most, if not all, financial planners.

Social Security rules state that the benefit amount a widow or widower receives is based on a percentage of the deceased spouse's benefit amount calculated at the time of retirement. (See Figure 5.4 for an overview of benefit reduction calculations.) In most cases, the benefits are as follows:

▶ A widow or widower generally receives 100 percent of the deceased spouse's benefit amount if the surviving spouse is at FRA or older.

▶ A widow or widower under 60 receives about 71 to 99 percent of the deceased spouse's benefit amount through their full retirement.

▶ A widow or widower with a child younger than age 16 receives 75 percent of the worker's benefit amount.

Although the basic SSA rules might seem pretty straightforward, some smart money management strategies are still available within the rule's boundaries. For example, if a spouse dies before reaching retirement age, the surviving spouse can start collecting on the deceased spouse's benefits as early as age 60 while letting their own benefit continue to grow. Or the surviving spouse may collect on their own record and delay collecting on the survivor's benefits until their 70th birthday to collect the highest benefit amount. If you remarry after age 60, your benefits will not be affected.

Even without inflation rises, a surviving spouse would collect 32 percent more in monthly benefits by letting the 8 percent yearly bonus accrue for four years (between age 66 and 70).

Returning to Work and Benefits

Sometimes circumstances force us to change our best laid plans or opportunities arise that you can't resist; for example, an opportunity to consult. In these cases, if you are under FRA and you return to the working world, SSA will automatically suspend payments after your income reaches an amount tied to your particular retirement benefit classification. If you are over FRA, you can decide to continue receiving your benefit or you can suspend the payments and begin earning 8 percent on your future benefit.

Retiring With Children Under 18

It's easy to spot evidence that many retirement-age Americans still have children under 18 years old. Just stand on the sidelines of a pre-teen or teenage sporting event and notice how many of the parents cheering their children on are in their 50s and even in their 60s.

The evidence is in statistics as well. In 1960, 72 percent of all adults 18 and older were married. Today, only 51 percent of adults in this age category are married, and according to research by the Pew Research Center, that number will soon dip below 50 percent. So clearly, we're marrying later and in many cases having children later in life.[7]

Working During Retirement

According to the Social Security Administration, the amount you can earn while receiving Social Security depends on your age. However, once you reach FRA your earnings won't affect your Social Security benefits. Here are the published SSA earnings rules:

Before Reaching Full Retirement Age
- You can earn $15,480 gross wages or net self-employment a year and not lose any benefits in 2014.
- SSA will deduct $1 in benefits for every $2 earned above $15,480.

After Reaching Full Retirement Age
- You can earn $41,400 gross wages or net self-employment prior to the month you reach full retirement age and not lose any benefits in 2014.
- SSA will deduct $1 in benefits for every $3 earned above $41,400.

The same earnings limits apply to a spouse or child who works and receives benefits.[8]

Figure 5.5

First, you should know that if you are eligible for benefits and have a dependent under 18 your dependent is eligible for benefits. This rule also applies to adopted children or stepchildren. Dependent grandchildren may also qualify for Social Security benefits if they are unmarried and less than 18 years old. Children over 18 also qualify if they are still in high school or were disabled before age 22.

The second important fact to know about retiring with dependents under 18 is that their benefits won't decrease your retirement benefit amount, but in fact may

Five-Star Tip: Think Strategically About Receiving Social Security Benefits

Here are two tips to maximize your Social Security benefits:

- Delay drawing on your Social Security benefits for as long as possible, at least until your full retirement age, and preferably until age 70, to collect the greatest monthly payments.

- Take advantage of spousal benefits in strategic ways (e.g., using a file-and-suspend strategy) to ensure your potential retirement benefits are maximized.

be the reason that you decide to claim retirement benefits earlier than you expected. However, a family maximum benefit and income limits do apply.

Benefits Paid and Limits

Each qualified dependent is entitled to receive a monthly payment up to one-half of your full retirement benefit amount. (The family maximum is generally about 150 to 180 percent of the claiming spouse's FRA benefit.) SSA income limit rules do apply to dependent income while they receive benefits, but any income they earn won't affect your benefits.

I often advise clients with dependents under 18 that when they reach 62 years old if one spouse is not working, to consider collecting their benefits early. While they are claiming early and getting a reduced benefit, the extra benefit on the child, if saved properly, can help offset college costs. Once the child reaches 18 and the nonworking spouse is at least FRA, but still under 70, suspend the benefits and allow growth to resume at 8 percent. It is also likely that in this situation the other spouse will work into their 70s so their benefit will enjoy the full growth in waiting to claim until age 70. The surviving spouse receives the greater of the two benefits.

What's Next and Wrap Up

Chapter 6 provides the guidance you need to make the best healthcare-planning decisions possible before and after your retirement. The chapter includes advice on choosing (or not choosing) among various long-term care insurance options as well as key strategies that will protect your larger pool of assets even as healthcare costs continue to rise.

Here's a recap of the key information presented in this chapter:

- ▶ Social Security benefits should be around until at least 2033 and very likely thereafter.

- ▶ Delay collecting Social Security benefits as long as you can (at least until age 70). Just a year or two makes a big difference because your benefits grow at 8 percent a year.

- ▶ Claiming spousal benefit adds extra income while waiting to claim your own retirement benefits.

- ▶ Because the first 15 percent of a benefit payment is tax-free, filing for benefits at 62 might be the right strategy for some single individuals to help them delay paying taxes on a retirement account with withdrawals.

- ▶ A file-and-suspend strategy allows one working spouse to delay claiming their own benefit but allows the spouse to collect a spousal benefit.

- ▶ Whether or not an 18-year-old and under dependent is biologically tied to you, your dependent can still claim Social Security benefits.

- ▶ If you were married to a spouse for at least 10 years and you are currently unmarried and not entitled to a higher benefit, you are eligible to receive benefits on that former spouse's record.

- ▶ It's possible to begin collecting the Social Security benefits of a spouse who died before they reached their retirement of 62. Benefits can even be delayed until the deceased spouse's 70th birthday to collect maximum benefits.

Put Aside Enough Money to Cover Healthcare

In This Chapter

▶ Determine a Reasonable Healthcare Budget

▶ Benefit from the Affordable Care Act

▶ Connect Your Planned Lifestyle and Healthcare

▶ Choose the Best Long-Term Care Plan

Planning for future healthcare expenses is a challenging guessing game with long odds on winning. That's why the best strategy—and perhaps the only strategy—is to build a comprehensive retirement plan that puts the odds of winning in your favor. This chapter is designed to help you make these savvy planning decisions. But first, here's a bit of history that may explain why healthcare is the most anxiety-producing aspect of retirement planning.

History of U.S. Healthcare

Prior to Franklin D. Roosevelt's New Deal initiatives in the early 1930s government-provided healthcare got little public attention and even less traction in Congress. But

Deadly Mistake #6

Underestimating Healthcare Costs

the 1929 Great Depression exposed a deep need for healthcare assistance among a vast number of impoverished and financially struggling Americans. It is interesting to note that one of Roosevelt's New Deal centerpieces, the legislation that created the Social Security Administration, originally included a provision for a publicly funded healthcare system. But a familiar coalition of interest groups—the American Medical Association, insurance companies, and others—forced Roosevelt to drop the provision.

For the next 30 years, various versions of publicly provided or supported healthcare initiatives were introduced in Congress or promised during political campaigns. Even President Harry Truman failed to get support for his 1949 Fair Deal program that called for a national healthcare system. It was not until 1965 when Lyndon Johnson passed Medicare and Medicaid legislation as part of his Great Society initiative that national healthcare programs of any kind were rolled out.

Why Do Healthcare Costs Scare Us?

A recent statistic published by NerdWallet.com shows that healthcare expenses drive more Americans into personal bankruptcy than even job loss or poor financial planning.[1]

The conclusions were based on an analysis of the U.S. Census, bankruptcy statistics, citizen behavioral data, and pharmaceutical use data.

Between 1965 and President Bill Clinton's unsuccessful 1993 attempt to pass healthcare legislation, successive presidents tinkered around the edges enacting legislative add-ons and patches to the existing Social Security law. One of these patches (first in 1974 and refined in 1985) was an add-on that allowed employees to keep their current health coverage after losing a job with coverage.

But it was not until the election of President Obama in 2008 that tackling the problem of healthcare took center stage again, although President George W. Bush did add his own legacy to healthcare reform with the passage of the Medicare Prescription Drug Improvement and Modernization Act of 2003 that provided drug-purchasing assistance for the elderly and disabled.[2]

Affordable Care Act

The ultimate effect of President Obama's signature on the cost of health insurance through the Affordable Care Act (ACA) legislation that passed in 2010 is still unclear even in early 2014 as this book is being written.

Even if the ACA completely succeeds and every American has access to an insurance plan they can afford and the spiraling healthcare costs are moderated for now, the fact remains that healthcare costs still have the potential to destroy financial security in retirement.

Current Healthcare Costs

Currently, the typical employer spends about $11,768 per year on premiums for every employee; the employees pay an average of $4,565 of the annual $16,000 cost. In 2003, the average per employee cost paid by the employer was $6,657; an employee contribution to the total bill was $2,412.[3]

Initial government estimates of the average cost of coverage provided by the ACA is about $338 per month.[4] That's slightly less than the average current monthly employee contribution of $380. But

Affordable Care Act Essentials

The Health Insurance Marketplace, a new way for individuals, families, and small businesses to get health coverage:

- requires insurance companies to cover people with pre-existing health conditions.

- helps you understand the coverage you're getting.

- holds insurance companies accountable for rate increases.

- makes it illegal for health insurance companies to arbitrarily cancel your health insurance just because you get sick.

- protects your choice of doctors.

- covers young adults, under 26.

- provides free preventive care.

- ends lifetime and yearly dollar limits on coverage of essential health benefits.

- guarantees your right to appeal.[5]

the actual price you'll pay for coverage under ACA varies by state and region and even the availability and choice of medical services in your home area.

However, the ACA does offer some provisions that may strengthen the hand of today's retirees and those approaching retirement age including the provision that prevents insurers from refusing to provide insurance due to a pre-existing condition (or to drop coverage due to a new condition). The ACA also removes the lifetime cap on most accumulated healthcare expenses. These two changes alone offer great potential to save you money by reducing the financial squeeze on your retirement assets should you have a major health crisis later in life.

Lifestyle and Healthcare Choices

Regardless of how the ACA ultimately affects your personal healthcare budget and the decisions you make about coverage, you'll still be faced with healthcare decisions that require you to balance the level of healthcare services you need and the lifestyle you want to live.

If you plan to move to another state or region after you retire, then it's absolutely essential to ensure that the health services you *need* or even *expect to need* are available at nearby medical facilities. Many regions of the country may have affordable housing but not the level of healthcare services you need. Second, check with your insurance carrier to ensure your plan is the same in the state or region you've targeted. Plans are typically restricted to the area where you live, so if your coverage is provided through your former employer it's a good idea to check coverage. Sometimes it's the easily overlooked terms and conditions that have the greatest effect on your coverage.

For example, some HMO plans restrict where you can move if you have certain conditions. One of my business associates told me that his mother-in-law was prevented from leaving her HMO-approved facility to seek treatment for cancer in another state. During the month-long process required to get this approval, his mother-in-law's condition worsened.

Medicare

Medicare is a federal health insurance program created by the Johnson administration in 1965[6] to assist Americans age 65 or older with paying for inpatient and outpatient hospital expenses as well as prescription drugs. Younger Americans with specific disabilities or medical conditions are also covered by this program. Medicaid is a joint federal and state program that helps those with limited income and re-sources pay for medical costs.[7]

Specifically, Medicare's coverage is divided into four parts: Part A (hospital insurance), Part B (medical insurance); Part C (advantage or additional benefits); and Part D (prescription drugs). Here's what is covered by each part:

Part A

If you or your spouse paid Medicare taxes during your working years, then this part of your coverage usually doesn't require payment of a monthly premium (typically in the form of a deduction from your monthly Social Security benefit check). Specifically, Part A covers:

▶ inpatient care in hospitals

▶ skilled nursing facility care

▶ hospice care

▶ home healthcare.

Part B

This coverage requires payment of a standard monthly premium. Many retirees buy an additional policy from a private insurer called a Medicare Supplement

---

Five-Star Tip: Don't Expect Your Children to Take Care of You

A generation ago, it was very common, almost expected, that one of your responsibilities as an adult was to take care of your parents in their old age. While I realize that there are many people who still take on this responsibility for love, duty, financial reasons, or a combination of all three reasons, my sense is that this care is less common today. Today's 50- and 60-year-olds are less likely to accept this responsibility for a lot of reasons that have more to do with their active, less home- and place-focused lives. The point is, if you expect your children—one more generation removed from these elder care traditions—to take care of you, think again.

Sure, they might do it, but I suspect they'd consider it not an optimal arrangement at best.

Insurance (Medigap) to fill in any payment gaps in the Medicare coverage. Part B covers:

▶ services from doctors and other healthcare providers

▶ outpatient care

▶ home healthcare

▶ durable medical equipment

▶ some preventive services.

Part C
This offers a way for retirees to buy their Part A and B coverage from Medicare-approved private insurance companies. The program, also called Medicare Advantage, usually includes Part D prescription coverage.

Part D
This provides prescription drug coverage through Medicare-approved private insurance companies. Part D pays a significant part of the cost of prescription drugs (or helps lower the cost) or protects against higher costs in the future.

Medicaid
Medicaid is a joint federal and state program aimed at those with limited income and resources. In addition to healthcare benefits, Medicaid also covers nursing home care, personal care services, and prescription drugs.[8]

Many people take advantage of Medicaid rules that allow those with too much income to still qualify for Medicaid by "spending down" to be medically needy so that they can qualify for coverage. Spending down is a process that subtracts

Assisted-living and Long-term Care Costs

	Nursing Homes		Assisted Living Communities	Home Care		Adult Day Services
	Semi-Private Room	Private Room		Home Health Aide	Homemaker	
Rate Type	Daily		Monthly	Hourly		Daily
2012 Avg. Rate	$222	$248	$3,550	$21	$20	$70
2011 Avg. Rate	$214	$239	$3,477	$21	$19	$70
$/% Increase from 2011	$8 (3.7%)	$9 (3.8%)	$73 (2.1%)	$0 (0%)	$1 (5.3%)	0 (0%)
2012 Annual Rate	$81,030	$90,520	$42,600	$21,840	$20,800	$18,200

Figure 6.1 Summary of National Findings – Costs are rounded off to the nearest dollar. Information provided by MetLife. Annual rates for home care are based on 4 hours per day, 5 days per week; annual rates for adult services are based on 5 days per week.

medical expenses from income to become medically needy, i.e., total income is below a certain threshold set by each state.

The Bottom-Line Benefit

So that's the overview of these essential retiree healthcare support programs. And here are a few more thoughts on the topic:

▶ If you have high medical expenses in retirement, you should be able to take more money out of your IRA at lower rates to help pay for these costs by using them as a deduction on your tax returns.

▶ If you have the opportunity to open a Health Savings Account while you're still working, sign up for it.

▶ Make sure you coordinate all of your benefits to pre-vent overlapping.

From Our Practice...
Happy Together

Everyone has heard of the expression "dying of a broken heart." It's one of those expressions we know is true just through life experience. Research studies even bear out this conventional wisdom, especially within a 30-day period after a spouse's death.

That's why I advise clients investigating assisted care to consider only those facilities with co-located long-term care options. It's a sad situation to plan for, but being able to easily visit the person you've shared your life with for the past 40 years must be a top consideration.

This is exactly what happened to a client and his wife. (I'll call them Bob and Anne.) The couple entered an upscale assisted-living facility in their mid-70s and spent the next 10 years traveling and enjoying their large network of friends. Then one day, Anne got lost walking back from a visit with a friend in the next building.

Sadly, five years later Anne needed full-time care in an associated nursing home just a short walk from Bob and Anne's apartment. Bob visited the woman he still called "the love of his life" every day even though Anne no longer recognized him. The arrangement allowed Bob to continue living his life without the stress of worry and concern about Anne's care. And it's probably why Bob lived well into his 90s despite the tragedy of Anne's condition.[9]

▶ Communicate your health-care plans with your family so they'll know what to expect.

Assisted-living and Long-Term Care

One of the major themes of this book is the potential for unexpected and unplanned expenses to quickly drain all of your retirement assets. Just the statistics I've provided in this book reveal why you should have a high level of concern. I cannot emphasize enough how critical it is to address the question of long-term care insurance in your retirement budget.

For example, the average cost of nursing-home care, assisted-living care, adult day services, and home care all increased dramatically in 2012 according to the *2012 MetLife Market Survey of Nursing Home, Assisted-living, Adult Day Services, and Home Care Costs*. The survey reported that the average yearly cost of a private room nursing home was $90,520 (or $248 a day).

The cost for a semi-private room averaged about $81,030 a year (or $222 a day). These costs are almost double the average cost of spending a year in an assisted-living facility: $42,600 or $3,550 a month (see Figure 6.1).

However, these are average costs. If you live in Washington, DC, you'll pay $121,910 a year in a private room in an assisted-living facility (or $5,933 a month). Alaska assisted-living rates are even higher, averaging an amazing $657 a day or $250,775 a year! In New York, the yearly cost is $134,320 while an average year's stay in an assisted-living facility in Minnesota is $87,965, and the same private room in California averages about $120,450 a year.[10]

Assisted-care Options

Depending on your state of health and financial ability, you'll find many options for assisted-living and long-term care. That's why it's important to make the wisest choice possible that specifically fits your needs.

> **Tips on Long-Term Care Insurance**
>
> - Make sure the company is highly rated and stable.
>
> - Remember, premium rates are not guaranteed and can go up for the whole group.
>
> - Carefully review the various inflation riders.
>
> - Check to ensure the policy covers home healthcare.
>
> - Think carefully about the benefit period of a policy. The typical long-term care need is three years so you can save money on the premiums for lifetime care benefits.

The types of facilities included in the assisted-living averages cited above range from fairly modest living arrangements to those with high-end amenities and services. According to the market forecasting company BCC Research, the current $46 billion industry is expected to grow to more than $60.5 billion by 2018.[11] Some facilities allow residents to buy their apartments and then pay a monthly resident fee that includes meals, cleaning, and other resident services. When the residents at these buy-in facilities move to a nursing home or die, their children or heirs sell the apartment for 80 to 90 percent of the original purchase price.

From Our Practice...

Healthcare for the Long-term

One of the key concepts in this book is that a surprising percentage of the population will live into their 90s. And yes, on many levels that is good news. But unfortunately, the gift of longer life must be balanced with two significant downsides. First, living longer means you'll need more assets to support everyday expenses for a longer period of time. Second, you'll probably also need enough assets to pay for assisted-living or nursing home care. My advice to anyone planning for these expenses is to seek out professional advice (especially with potential changes that may happen as a result of the Affordable Care Act). Here is an example to consider:

The mother of a client I saw was advised to cut her overall living expenses by taking the least expensive, but also most restrictive, healthcare plan. The plan was fine until my client's mother had a condition that required the help of a doctor practicing outside of her home state. My client said that by the time his mother had gone through the required process to get the change approval—a period of several months—his mother's condition was more difficult to treat and the delay ultimately shortened her life.

A number of our clients have chosen to buy into a facility, and if the heirs are able to sell the apartment at a reasonable percentage of the original cost, then I will often advise them to follow that path. Ask your financial planner or tax advisor for advice specific to your own financial situation and retirement goals.

Even if you don't buy into a facility, I advise my clients—particularly couples—to do their best to find assisted-living with a nursing-care facility associated with it. If one of the spouses encounters a debilitating health issue, making a short trip to the next building or across an assisted-living campus is a much better option for regular visits than traveling across town, especially when driving is no longer an option for a spouse. Remember, you have a good chance of living until you're 90 years old, so this is a contingency well worth thinking about.

As noted, assisted-living facilities vary greatly in costs, amenities, and services, depending on where you live. And unfortunately, the care you get is greatly dependent on the price paid. That's why I emphasize to my clients the importance of planning to spend a sufficient amount on these services. So how is that goal accomplished?

First, if you are fortunate enough to have $5 million or more in your retirement and non-retirement accounts, and a retirement package that includes health insurance, then you can probably afford to self-insure your stay at the assisted-living facility of your choice. However, for the rest of us, a little more comprehensive planning is required.

Long-Term Care Insurance

Like many decisions in life, the answer to whether you should purchase a long-term health insurance policy at any age comes down to available cash flow. Someone in an established, stable marriage with the financial flexibility to afford it might take advantage of discounts and sign up at the next yearly company benefits fair. Someone single with less cash is likely to walk past this benefits booth. As a general rule, the best time to buy this type of insurance is in your mid-50s and early 60s. And remember, if you do sign up for group coverage, make sure it's portable.

It may be true that saving enough money for healthcare is difficult to gauge, but it's still possible to win this guessing game. After all, the prize for winning with good planning is the ability to live a great life, retire financially secure, have a second great act, and then leave the stage of life with dignity.

What's Next and Wrap Up

Chapter 7 will help you take advantage of money-saving tax breaks and deductions. The tips range from taking dividends and capital gains as cash to bundling medical expenses to smart ways to pay your Medicare taxes.

Here's a recap of the key information presented in this chapter:

▶ On average Americans pay about $380 a month for health insurance if they're covered under their employer's policy. You might pay more or less once the Affordable Care Act is fully implemented. Stay tuned. The government announced the average cost is $328 a month.

▶ If you plan to move to another state, do your due diligence to make sure that healthcare coverage is the same and all services are available in the state or region you've targeted.

▶ The average cost of a private room in a nursing home is about $90,520 a year.

▶ If you live in New York, the average yearly cost of nursing home care is $134,320 a year.

▶ The most expensive nursing-home care is in Alaska. You'll spend $657 a day on average in an Alaskan nursing facility, or $250,775 a year.

▶ Purchasing long-term care insurance is not for everybody, but buying it typically makes sense for someone in their mid-50s or early 60s.

Don't Pay More Taxes Than You Owe

In This Chapter

▶ Minimize Taxes With an Income Plan

▶ Manage Your Tax Bracket to Save Money

▶ Cut Taxes by Donating Appreciated Stock

▶ Reduce Tax Burden Using Smart Strategies

Everyone pays taxes. It's the price we all pay for the privilege of living in a safe, functioning society with publicly funded roads, bridges, schools, and all of the other services we take for granted as American citizens. But that doesn't mean we shouldn't take advantage of every available tax break if it helps to check off items on a retirement bucket list or pass down some of our hard-earned assets to children and other heirs.

This chapter offers some key strategies to ensure that you pay only the taxes you owe and not a dime more. I'll show you why taking dividends and capital gains as cash is a smart money move, how bundling medical expense deductions saves money, and how to structure Medicare payments in cash-saving ways. You'll also find advice on how to reduce

Deadly Mistake #7

Overpaying Taxes

your tax liability through shifting assets (such as cash and appreciated stock) to your children. But first let's review why a retirement income plan is an important part of this tax-reduction strategy.

Create an Income Plan to Minimize Taxes

The purpose of a retirement income plan is to identify all potential sources of income and then determine the best, most tax efficient way to draw on your saved assets. Depending on the complexity and number of potential income sources, it's fairly easy to get a rough idea of your potential monthly income.

First, there's Social Security and pension income. If you don't have a copy of your latest projected benefits sent out by the Social Security Administration, then go to the SSA website (www.ssa.gov) and set up an account. Once you've registered, the benefit information for any retirement scenario you might imagine is readily available.

Next, gather up the current value of 401(k) and other retirement and nonretirement assets such as stocks, bonds, annuities, and any other potential income source (including rental property income). The idea is to determine a total cash flow potential that you can compare to your best estimate of projected retirement expenses. (See Figure 7.1 for a sample income plan.)

Here are some income plan line items you're likely to list.

▶ Fixed Sources of Income

Fixed-income sources are stable and predictable sources such as Social Security benefits, pension, and annuity income as well as any expected earnings from part-time or seasonal work. You would also list any rental property income as a fixed-income source.

▶ Retirement and Nonretirement Assets

Retirement and nonretirement assets include your 401(k), Roth IRA, stocks, bonds, or other dividend and interest revenue. The income you derive from

Monthly Income Sources

1. Employment	Self	Spouse
Gross Salary		
Bonuses, incentive pay, etc.		
Unemployment benefits		
Pension benefits		
Miscellaneous		

2. Interest and Dividends		
Checking and savings account interest		
Investment dividends and interest		

3. Other Income		
Retirement account distributions**		
Beneficiary IRA distributions		
Annuities (annuitized or immediate)		
Social Security benefits		
Consulting income		
Trust-fund income		
Alimony/Child support		
Rental property income		
Mortgage payments (incoming)		
Parental/relative gifts (ongoing)		
Royalties		
Miscellaneous		
Total Gross Income		

4. Income Taxes	Self	Spouse	Business*
Federal income taxes			
State income taxes (if applicable)			
Local income taxes (if applicable)			
Social Security taxes (if applicable)			
Payroll taxes (if applicable)			

NET INCOME			

** Required Monthly Deductions (RMD) from Traditional IRAs must begin at age 70-1/2
    Roth IRAs – no distributions required

Figure 7.1

Net Investment Income Tax

The income received on investment earnings before tax is called net investment income. This includes bonds, stocks, mutual funds, loans, rental income, and other investments—after subtracting related expenses.

these assets requires careful management and the use of specific strategies such as the ones discussed in this chapter and the next chapter on estate planning.

▶ *Plan for the Medicare Tax*

The federal government levies a tax that averages about 2.9 percent on the wages you earn either through an employer or as a result of self-employment. If you're employed in a company, then your employer picks up half the cost (1.45 percent) and you pick up the other half.

If you're self-employed, then you're responsible for the entire 2.9 percent, but IRS rules do allow you to take a deduction for one-half of the Medicare tax you pay (1.45 percent) as part of self-employment tax when you file your personal income tax returns. And one last fact to keep in mind about this tax: unlike Social Security tax which has a limit, there is no limit on Medicare tax.

In 2013 (as part of Affordable Care Act implementation) high-income single tax-payers with incomes above $200,000 and those married and filing jointly with income more than $250,000 were required to pay an extra 0.9 percent of employment income tax on top of a new 3.8 percent net investment income tax (see sidebar).

Earnings on individual IRAs and Roth IRAs are technically not subject to this additional tax. However, certain income scenarios could require payment of additional taxes based on defined IRS threshold amounts. For example, if an IRA withdrawal of $30,000 was required during a given year when investment income was $240,000, the additional income over $250,000 or $20,000 (assuming a joint filing) would be subject to the 3.8 percent tax plus the additional 0.9 percent tax. Any nonqualified annuity income would also be subject to this tax.[1]

Self-employed and business owners have the largest potential to be affected by this change. One strategy to avoid this tax is to simply manage the modified adjusted gross income so that the reported income does not exceed the new threshold amounts. For example, income might be deferred into a 401(k) or other retirement plan and, thus, reduce reported income enough to avoid this tax.

Use Appreciated Securities for Charitable Contributions

First, a definition. A qualified appreciated stock is any publicly traded stock that on the day of its contribution could be sold for a long-term capital gain benefit. That's a pretty broad definition so most of the stocks you're likely to own qualify for this strategy. The advantage of donating appreciated stock includes:

▶ an immediate fair market–value income tax deduction based on the date of transfer regardless of the original cost of the stock

▶ no capital gains tax implication for the individual donor (the charity is subject to the gain but will owe no income taxes)

▶ the donation will maximize the value of your gift to the cause or charity.

Imagine that you want to give the college you attended a $20,000 cash gift. You own 400 shares of a stock that you bought for $2,000 a few years ago, and it is now worth $20,000 (a 10-fold increase in value). Selling the stock outright and gifting the proceeds as cash would mean you'd pay $4,284 in capital gains tax (assuming a 20 percent long-term tax rate plus the 3.8 percent net investment income tax on your gain of $18,000). So in the end, you'd be able to contribute $15,716 to the college.

However, if you gave appreciated stock, the college would get the entire $20,000 market value of the stock while you'd avoid capital gains tax and enjoy a tax-reducing benefit. A few important caveats about giving appreciated stock:

▶ If you've held an appreciated security for less than one year and one day, only the cost basis is deductible, i.e., the original value adjusted for stock splits, dividends, and return of capital distributions.

▶ If the stock has lost value, the best strategy is to sell the stock, claim the loss on your tax returns, and donate the resulting cash.

Benefit from Smart Tax Strategies

▶ *Bunch Medical Expenses*

It's just a fact of life that our medical expenses increase as we age. But bunching medical expenses can be a smart strategy to reduce your annual tax liability both before and after retirement.

Essentially, bunching medical expenses means prepaying (or pushing off) medical expenses to take advantage of an IRS rule that allows medical expenses to be deducted from your gross income if these expenses exceed 10 percent of your adjusted gross income (AGI). The rate is 7.5 percent if you're over age 65. (Note: Prior to 2013 and the enactment of the Affordable Care Act, the threshold amount was 7.5 percent).

Here's how you might use this rule. If one dependent (a child) had significant medical expenses in 2013 and another dependent was scheduled to get braces in early 2014, you add both expenses together and the expense might exceed 10 percent of your AGI. If this were the case, it would have made sense to prepay the orthodontist for the dental work in 2013 and take the tax benefit. Remember that this strategy is intended for discretionary or unreimbursed expenses. Clearly if a medical condition requires immediate attention, no matter the potential savings, then this would not be an appropriate strategy.

▶ *Take Dividends and Capital Gains as Cash*

Before you retired, you likely allowed any dividend income you received to be reinvested to build your position with that investment. However, when you retire the best strategy is to take dividends from your nonretirement assets as cash and incorporate the money into your regular cash flow. This is the right strategy because it avoids incurring capital gains tax later on if you need cash for living expenses. It also builds up your asset reserves so that you'll have options to maintain your needed cash flow other than selling assets when the market is down.

▶ *Shift Asset to Children to Minimize Tax*

If you plan to give money to children or grand-children, one way to do so while getting a tax ben-efit is to give them a stock that has grown since you bought it. The strategy is similar to the one used for charitable giving. Of course, your family member will pay the capital gains tax when they sell the asset, but that tax is based on the recipi-ent's tax bracket, unless a dependent and subject to the kiddie tax (see sidebar). That's why this is a good strategy to pass down assets to heirs in lower tax brackets who might need the cash to pay off student loans or other early career or life needs.

▶ *Use Tax Loss Harvesting*

Tax loss harvesting is a common technique used to reduce the amount of capital gains you have to pay when cashing out portions of a portfolio to access the proceeds from profitable trades. In practical terms, tax loss harvesting simply means balancing your investment gains against loss-es to limit the capital gains tax. Savvy investors and financial professionals use this technique for both short- and long-term gains, but the taxes paid on short-term gains are higher than the amount paid on long-term gain. So, if timed correctly, you or your investment advisor can use this technique to apply a $2,000 loss on one stock to a $2,000 gain on another stock so that your tax liability paid is a net gain of 0 percent.

For example, say you sold out of a position on an investment in June that you felt had run its course (or you just needed cash) and you realized a gain in the transaction. Then later on in the year you sell an underperforming position and realize a loss.

About the Kiddie Tax

The kiddie tax is an IRS rule that allows children to receive unearned income up to $2,000 (that's the threshold amount for 2014). The first $1,000 is tax free, the second $1,000 is taxed at the child's rate (usually 10%). However, any income received above this threshold amount is taxed at their parent's highest income tax rate.

Note that this rule applies only to unearned income a child receives from cash, stocks, bonds, mutual funds, or income-producing real estate property or investment. The kiddie tax applies to children under age 19 and children between the ages of 19 and 23 who are full-time students with limited earned income (50% of the annual cost for their support).

From Our Practice...
Pay Only the Taxes You Owe

Regardless of political leanings, no one likes to pay taxes. Still, most of us dutifully file our tax returns by April 15th even with our complaints about the system. When my clients express similar frustrations about their own tax liability, I give the only reasonable advice a financial expert can offer: just make sure you pay all of the taxes you owe, but not a penny more.

Ensuring that level of tax payment precision isn't easy, but sometimes clients don't recognize large tax-saving options right in front of them.

For example, a referral from a client sold a long-held beach front property in 2009. Of course, the value of this property had grown significantly over the years so that the client faced a considerable tax bill. He complained to me about having to pay taxes on his property's gain. At the same time he was facing the unhappy news that the value of a long-held stock investment had dropped from $60 per share to less than $1 per share. However, the client was happier with the situation when he learned how the investment loss could be used to balance his gains so that in the end, the tax liability for the sale of his beach house would be negligible.

By matching the gain and the loss, you'll avoid capital gains tax on the net gain.

Roth Conversion Filing after Age 70

Roth IRAs are useful investments that allow gains to accumulate over time, but assets can be withdrawn tax-free (that's because applicable taxes are paid when the Roth is initially funded).

So, let's say you have a $2 million IRA and at age 70-1/2 you need to start taking required distributions of around $70,000 a year. If you are currently in the 10 percent tax bracket because you're living mainly off Social Security income, the new income from your IRA would bump up your tax bracket to 25 percent. By converting portions of the IRA to a Roth IRA during the low-income years, you would

- pay less on taxes or the conversions
- potentially have a lower required minimum distribution (RMD) on your traditional IRA assets (Note: a Roth IRA does not have a RMD requirement).

Gifting Children or Grandchildren

In the next chapter, you will learn about the strategy of gifting cash to your children or grandchildren so they can max out their own existing IRA and fund their own retirement. Essentially, a couple filing jointly can gift up to $28,000 ($14,000 per spouse) to their children each year and use that contribution to reduce taxable income. I'll also discuss how to fund an educational 529 plan for heirs and why these and other estate-planning techniques can help you reduce your tax burden.

Other Gifting Techniques

Chapter 8 discusses a wide range of estate-planning techniques that will also affect the taxes you pay. Some of these techniques were discussed briefly in this chapter, but are expanded in the context of estate planning. These techniques include:

▶ gifting a Roth IRA

▶ gifting heirs through a 401(k) or 529 plan contribution

▶ giving appreciated stock to heirs and charity

▶ establishing a life insurance trust

▶ setting up a qualified personal residence trust.

Gifting for Businesses

Successful businesses, particularly family-owned ones, can also use gifting strategies to reduce taxes and pass down a financial legacy to the next generation. This is especially effective if stock is gifted early on in a company's life. Here's an example of this gifting strategy.

ABC Shoe Company is a company created to offer custom-made, high-end golf shoes. The idea catches on, and within five years the company has 125 employees with a market capitalization of $50 million. The company's board endorses a plan to take the company public (although there may be a better value attached if the company remains privately held) with shares offered at $10 each. Five thousand shares of the stock are put into an irrevocable trust for heirs. Within 10 years, that $50,000 gift is worth $5 million because the company's golf shoes are now worn by all of the top golf pros around the world. The heirs not only get a highly valued

Five-Star Tip: Bunch Medical Expenses for Tax Savings

When possible, bunch medical expenses to reduce tax liability. This strategy takes advantage of an IRS rule that allows a tax deduction for medical expenses if these costs exceed 10% of your adjusted gross income—the rate is 7.5% if you're 65 or older. If your medical expenses fall short of this benchmark, try prepaying enough medical expenses to help you meet this threshold. For example, one of my clients had a medical condition that required taking a drug not covered by Medicare.We used the $30,000 cost of the drug to significantly reduce his tax liability because it exceeded 7.5% of his gross retirement income.

stock, but they also get their inheritance without paying estate taxes.

Of course, that's just one of many ways that estates can be gifted to heirs to avoid paying estate taxes. And as you'd imagine, all come with various upsides and downsides. For example, in the scenario I just gave, the heirs would lose direct control of the asset because the estate trustee controls the purse strings.

Here's another strategy to use. Assume that three children are part of a FLP for a company worth $1 million in 2014. The wife would gift $28,000 to each child, but because the children are limited partners, the gift would be discounted. Again, you should seek appropriate legal advice to make sure this strategy is right for your particular situation.

What's Next and Wrap Up

Chapter 8 provides additional techniques to maintain your retirement cash flow while reducing taxes and preserving as much of your assets as possible for your heirs. While the area of estate planning is complex, I do provide key ways to avoid legal and financial complications that should be part of every trust and inheritance management strategy.

Here's a recap of the key information presented in this chapter:

▶ Create an income plan that provides all of the cash you need in retirement while at the same time reducing your annual tax burden and preserving assets for your heirs.

▶ High-income individuals (who are often business owners) pay higher Medicare taxes under the Affordable Care Act.

▶ High-income individuals (those with net investment income of more than $250,000 for a married couple, $200,000 for a single taxpayer, and $125,000 for married individuals but filing separately) owe an additional .09 percent tax beginning in 2013 above the standing 3.8 tax rate.

▶ Gifting appreciated stock to a charity allows a tax deduction for the donor equal to the fair market value of the donated stock and allows the designated charity to have access to the full value of the donated assets without paying income tax.

▶ Take dividends as cash, and incorporate the money into your regular cash flow because it avoids incurring capital gains tax and builds up your asset reserves.

▶ Prepay medical expenses to take advantage of a tax deduction for medical expenses if doing so means you'll meet the threshold amount of more than 10 percent of your adjusted gross income.

▶ Directly gifting cash to your children up to the maximum allowable amount can reduce your taxable income by $28,000.

Plan an Estate
That Will Enable Your Heirs

In This Chapter

▶ Choose the Right Trustee

▶ Set Up an Irrevocable or Revocable Trust

▶ Use Smart Strategies to Maximize Your Financial Legacy

▶ Motivate and Enable Your Heirs

▶ Transition Family Businesses

In the last chapter, you learned about using smart tax-code strategies to reduce the taxes you pay and how these savings ultimately affect achieving your retirement goals. This chapter digs a little deeper into long-term retirement planning strategies that benefit your positive cash flow today while preserving the value of the assets you will eventually pass on to your heirs.

Estate law complexity is rivaled only by the sheer volume and scope of U.S. tax law, so the discussion offered in this chapter is limited to some of the more

Disclaimer: The information in this chapter does not constitute legal advice. Please see a qualified and experienced estate planning attorney for advice on your specific situation.

Deadly Mistake #8

Lack of Succession Planning

applicable strategies that relate to retirement planning. To this practical end, the first part of this chapter sets the basic context for the discussion while the remaining pages guide you in making the right legal and financial decisions to support this goal of steady retirement cash flow and your financial legacy.

What Is a Trust?

A trust is a legal framework that allows a third party to hold your property until it can be transferred to your beneficiaries. After you pass on, this third party—called a trustee—ensures that your final wishes are communicated to your heirs and that your estate's financial matters are administered according to your wishes. Needless to say, the trustee you appoint must be someone you absolutely trust.

Depending on the trust type (see the discussion that follows on revocable and irrevocable trusts), setting up a trust provides a number of tangible and intangible benefits:

▶ significant tax savings for you and your beneficiaries

▶ limited or complete control of how and when your heirs will have access to your financial legacy

▶ assurance that a trusted party will carry out your explicit wishes

▶ protects your estate from potential creditor claims.

In addition, a trustee is someone you trust to manage and mediate potential family conflicts over your estate's assets and their disbursement. And as discussed later in the chapter, a trustee's job can even extend to ensuring that your financial legacy enables your heirs to lead successful lives.

Choosing the Right Trustee

Because your chosen trustee plays such a critical role in the disbursement of your financial legacy, here is a key consideration for choosing a trusted trustee:

Does the trustee have your absolute confidence and trust? This is an obvious question, and in some respects, it is the same benchmark you might use to choose a bank. However, the standard for choosing a trustee goes beyond just a well-documented record of ethical conduct and customer service. As your only spokesperson, you must have confidence that your trustee will carry out your wishes exactly as proscribed. Remember, as much as we'd all like to direct our own beneficiary meeting, this is definitely not a meeting we can attend. You may also decide to hire a trust company to name as trustee or co-trustee to ensure your wishes are followed.

The need to have this higher level of trust is why a family member is often appointed as trustee. For some, a longtime business associate or close, lifelong friend is the right choice. Still others, due to family dynamics or the size and complexity of the estate, choose to hire someone with the right level of professional or legal expertise to handle the job. But no matter who ends up handling your estate—whether a family member, friend, or professional trust company—it's imperative to choose someone who will reflect your wishes and not allow personal opinions, pre-existing loyalties, and biases to cloud the decisions they make.[1]

Still, circumstances sometimes demand compromise. Here are a few circumstances that might force you to seek a middle ground:

High Asset Value

▶ A high value trust or a trust with a complex asset structure will probably require hiring a trust expert. You'll pay fees for these services, but the cost is worth it, especially if the trust involves asset distribution to multiple generations and other complicated or milestone-driven distribution requirements such as a requirement for a beneficiary to complete college or reach a certain age before having access to the trust assets.

Poor Family Relationships

▶ Unfortunately, not all families enjoy harmonious relationships, and even if family members do trust or like each other, money—especially substantial amounts of money held in a trust—often has a way of trumping a lifetime of positive family relationships.

Some reliable indicators that trust distribution troubles are ahead include situations in which the estate owner or intended beneficiaries have gone through several marriages. Even if reasonable steps are taken as old marriages are dissolved and new marriages are begun (including the signing of prenuptial agreements), it's a good idea to appoint a smart, dispassionate estate professional to referee potential challenges to your specific trust disbursement wishes.

But no matter whom you designate as your trustee, you'll need to apply a few common-sense rules:

▶ *Choose a trustee with a reasonable chance of living long beyond your own demise.* If your first trustee choice is 80 years old and in poor health, you'd be wise to find a younger, healthier candidate despite qualities such as fairness, experience, and wisdom. Even if you choose a younger and healthier trustee, you'll need to choose a backup or successor trustee just in case your first choice dies or is unable to take on the responsibility due to a medical condition or debilitating accident.

▶ *Revisit your trust and trustee choice.* Just because you set up a trust and appointed a trustee when you were 65 years old as part of the retirement planning process, that doesn't mean you can forget about this important family responsibility. Life circumstances change over time, and decisions you made about your trust 5 or 10 years ago are very likely to change. For example, you might have a change of heart about limiting asset access to a beneficiary who has grown to be more responsible over the last five years.[2]

Irrevocable and Revocable Trusts

Setting up a trust and naming a trustee allows you to refine the role and responsibilities of a trustee and direct in very specific ways how and when beneficiaries may access trust assets. The two types of trusts, irrevocable and revocable, are somewhat defined by their names, but, as you'll see, each has specialized uses depending on the assets managed by the trust. A revocable trust, either living or testamentary, should be used even if there is no estate tax – if you want to guarantee assets don't go to the family or a remarried spouse.

In general, unless your estate's value (including insurance or death benefits) is in the neighborhood of $5 million, you probably won't need to set up an irrevocable trust, so you'll be able to take advantage of disbursement options such as timed distribution to beneficiaries (i.e., asset distributions yearly, quarterly, or at age 30). That's because estates valued above $5.34 million for single individuals and $10.68 million for married couples are subject to a hefty 40 percent estate tax. Irrevocable trusts offer more options to ameliorate this tax burden than a revocable trust. A surviving spouse must file IRS form 706 federal estate tax return in order to get the possible combined $10.68 million benefit. (Note: This is the lifetime estate tax exemption amount for 2014, and it's somewhat of a magic number for trust and estate professionals trying to save money for their clients and the clients' trust beneficiaries.)[3]

While a revocable trust does not provide any estate tax savings per se, a revocable trust does offer some powerful money- and time-saving incentives for just about everyone regardless of the value of the estate. A revocable trust becomes irrevocable upon death.

Irrevocable Trusts

Essentially, once an asset or property is established in an irrevocable trust you no longer control or own the assets. Despite this frightening-sounding aspect, an irrevocable trust offers some present-day tax advantages as well as a significantly reduced estate tax bill for your beneficiaries.

First, assets held in an irrevocable trust are not considered a taxable part of your estate. And because you no longer own the assets kept in an irrevocable trust, creditors cannot place a lien on the assets nor can irresponsible heirs access their inheritance and squander it foolishly. Even if all beneficiaries are as responsible as an accountant, it's a good idea to limit access (especially if the estate is large) through timed distributions. You might limit beneficiary access until a beneficiary reaches a specific age (e.g., 25 or 30 years old). You might also time distributions beginning at age 25 and continue distributions every five years until age 50 or 55. When the age threshold is reached, your heir or beneficiary would have full access to the assets.

The legal underpinnings of an irrevocable trust can be fairly complicated, and it wouldn't serve much value here. What's important to know is that the real-world results of setting up an irrevocable trust are often quite dramatic, but to take advantage of these benefits you'll need the savvy advice of a legal or financial expert familiar with the laws that govern them.

Revocable Trusts

Revocable trusts, as the name implies, allow for changes to be made in the trust terms during your life. The other benefit is that assets held in a revocable trust are not considered part of the donor's probate estate, and this can mean lower fees and avoiding time-consuming procedural hurdles (see sidebar).

What all of this means in practical terms is that when you pass on, your trustee will be able to quickly disburse estate assets to beneficiaries including any investment account assets, bank accounts assets, or properties such as your home. The main caveat here is to make sure that your attorney includes all of your assets in the revocable trust because any oversight, no matter how small, can mean a potentially costly and time-consuming trip to probate court.

Here is a real-life scenario that demonstrates the benefits of a revocable trust:

Sam Johnson and his wife, Sarah, worked hard and lived responsibly during their 40 years of marriage. Sam loved his job as an architect and always invested 10 to 15 percent of his salary in a company-sponsored 401(k) plan. Sarah worked for a local car dealership as an accountant where she also invested at least 10 percent of her salary in the dealership's 401(k) plan. By the time they retired at 65, they had accumulated a substantial amount of money to travel, pursue lifelong hobbies, and visit their grandchildren who lived 3,000 miles away in Los Angeles.

Over the next 25 years, Sam and Sarah had a great life traveling, entertaining friends, planning weddings for their two daughters, and taking their grandchildren on special vacations. Sam even designed and built a small house on a plot of land they owned at a nearby lake.

Then, right before his 89th birthday, Sam had a stroke and almost died before Sarah got him to the hospital. He survived, but the resulting paralysis meant he needed constant care at a nursing home. When Sam died a year later right after his 90th birthday, Sarah's health soon failed, and she died two years later at age 91 in the same nursing home that had cared for Sam.

Ten years before Sam had his stroke, he and Sarah worked with an attorney to set up a revocable trust so that they could begin transferring assets such as their home, lake house property and bank

What Is Probate?

Probate is a legal process used to administer estate distributions specified in a will and in some cases used to determine a will's validity. Going through the probate process is often expensive because the process can involve legal fees and other associated court costs. That's why it's highly advisable to avoid probate by setting up a trust and transferring ownership of your assets to beneficiaries named in the trust before you pass on. Note that probate costs vary significantly between states.

account to their trust so that when they passed these assets would go to their children, Dawn and Grace. Their oldest daughter, Dawn, was made the estate's executor and given financial power of attorney.

While Sarah was in the nursing home, Dawn took care of her mother's financial affairs. She was not surprised by the meticulous records her mother had kept, nor was she surprised by the final financial legacy her parents eventually left behind.

Now, just two weeks after saying goodbye to her mother, Dawn was sitting at her family kitchen table preparing an asset list for her sister. If her sister agreed with her accounting, she'd be able to close out the CD account the next day at her mom's bank and give Grace her portion of the account when they met for coffee at the local diner the next morning. She'd also be able to bring along the legal documents transferring 50 percent ownership of Sam and Sarah's stock holdings. Settling up the 401(k), Dawn decided, could wait until the next week, but she knew that process would be just as painless.

Because both the family home and the lake house property were included in the trust, Dawn and Grace were now the owners. The sisters had already discussed the properties and had decided to sell these assets later when the market improved. As for the open checking account, Dawn told her sister she'd keep the banking account open to pay property taxes and maintenance on the family home and lake house until they were sold.

The next morning at the local coffee shop, Grace gave Dawn a check she'd collected earlier from the bank. Grace was surprised, "Wow, I thought this would take a long time to sort out." Dawn laughed. "You know Mom. She was very smart about avoiding complications and saving money. She and Dad put everything they owned in a trust and transferred ownership to us, so that we'd avoid probate. Otherwise, we'd likely be having this meeting about six months from now and the check I just handed you would be much smaller.

Actually, Grace was absolutely correct about planning. Every year I hear numerous sad stories in which poor trust planning has resulted in assets intended for one family member go to a family member not specifically identified in the trust (for example, a family member's new spouse or new child). If drafted properly, the trust could protect your assets from being diverted to a surviving spouse's new family. You must make absolutely certain that your trust clearly reflects your wishes.

Grace smiled. "Well, all I can say is thanks, Mom," she said. "And by the way, you were right. He who plans ahead, really does stay ahead!"

Strategizing Estate and Trust Gifting

The narrative above illustrates how a great number of us use a trust to protect the financial legacy we leave behind for our heirs. Based on the sister's comments about their mother, it's likely that Sarah and and Sam used some of the techniques offered in this book to ensure that they'd leave something behind for their daughters.

Depending on your own financial situation, the estate-planning strategies that follow are some you'll likely use to ensure your own financial legacy is preserved for the next generation. These strategies include:

▶ offering annual cash gifts to children

▶ contributing to a 529 plan for children, grandchildren or even great-grandchildren

▶ establishing a Roth IRA

▶ giving appreciated stock to heirs or to a charity

▶ establishing a life insurance trust

▶ setting up a qualified personal residence trust.

Some of the strategies are more appropriate for irrevocable trusts than a revocable trust. As noted, one of the biggest challenges large estate holders face is keeping their estates below the $5.34 million to avoid a 40 percent estate tax levy.[4] By the way, it's worth mentioning that fewer than 2 out of every 1,000 Americans are in a financial position to owe any federal estate tax due to exceeding this large estate-exemption amount.

Gifting Annual Cash

The simple transfer of cash to children and other heirs is a standard tax-reduction strategy used by many financial planning professionals. Cash gifting ultimately reduces the potential tax liability associated with the estate you pass

How a 529 Investment Grows

Investing in a 529 plan for future use by a grandchild can result in a substantial educational legacy.

Here's how the funds might grow if invested over the grandchild's lifetime:

Investment: $14,000 per year beginning at birth

Return Rate: 8 percent annually

Value to Grandchild at age 18: $524,303

(Note: Total value is considered outside your estate for estate tax purposes and the growth income is tax-free if used for educational purposes by heirs.)

along to your heirs. A single individual can give up to $14,000 per year to as many individuals as they wish while a married couple can give up to $28,000 per year. The income tax on the gift's gains are paid by the recipient when assets are sold. The advantage of this cash gifting is that it reduces your estate and, therefore, reduces the potential that an estate-tax liability might fall to your heirs.

Establishing a 529 Plan

529 plans are the go-to college-saving fund for most Americans. Since the fund was established in 1996, the way 529 plans are used in estate planning has expanded. For example, grandparents wishing to leave a tax-free 529 educational legacy for an individual grandchild can gift the yearly maximum cash gift of $28,000 (per couple). Even better, if a set of grandparents are in a financial position to use recent tax-rule changes, they can use a lump-sum contribution of five times the federal government's annual gift-tax exclusion amount of $28,000 as noted above. (See sidebar for an example of the potential value.)

This means that a grandparent or parent with the resources to make the contribution can fund a 529 plan with a lump-sum gift of $70,000 to $140,000 every five years. For these individuals, this lump-sum contribution may be just the right amount of value reduction needed to keep an estate below the tax-free estate benchmark of $5.34 million for single individuals or $10.68 million for married couples. For the beneficiary, a yearly gift of $14,000 over the course of 15 or 20 years would represent quite a substantial tax-free educational legacy for the next generation.

In addition to this educational legacy for future generations, these contributions are transferred directly into the beneficiary's estate so the donor avoids paying any applicable estate taxes. And as long as the funds are used to pay qualified educational expenses, the withdrawals are also completely tax-free.

However, if the funds are withdrawn by the beneficiary and used for anything other than education-related expenses, a stiff ordinary income tax plus 10 percent penalty tax is imposed on the growth. Despite this potential downside, this gifting strategy makes sense for more affluent individuals who want both the tax benefits

The Fortunate Grandchild – How a $200,000 Roth Can Ultimately Grow to $1 Million

So how might the gift of a Roth IRA eventually turn into nearly a $1 million inheritance for a grandchild?

First, assume that the grandparent is about 75 years old, has a traditional IRA worth about $200,000, and doesn't necessarily need the money to pay expenses. However, due to minimum distribution rules based on life expectancy, the grandparent would be forced to take out nearly $15,000 from the traditional IRA and pay taxes on that amount unless a different strategy was devised; for example, a strategy of rolling over a traditional IRA to a Roth IRA.

Second, assume that the grandparent is very fond of a certain grandchild who is about five years old. After the grandparent passes on, the favored heir inherits the Roth IRA tax-free because the grandparent's worth is under $5.34 million. Here's how the gift grows assuming a 5% annual growth rate.

YEAR 1
Value of Inherited Roth IRA ~ $200,000
Minimum Distribution ~ $2,597
($200,000 divided by 77 years expected longevity)

YEAR 20
Value of Inherited Roth IRA ~$413,000
Minimum Distribution ~ $7,120
($413,000 divided by 58 years expected longevity)

YEAR 45
Value of Inherited Roth IRA ~$815,000
Minimum Distribution ~ $23,970
($815,000 divided by 34 years expected longevity)

YEAR 60
Value of Inherited Roth IRA ~$978,000
Minimum Distribution ~ $48,900
($978,000 divided by 20 years expected longevity)

The bottom line: the favored grandchild ends up with a retirement fund of nearly $1 million that grew tax-free over a 60-year period. However, the value is even more when you factor in all of the distributions the grandchild has taken over those years. Between the age of 5 and 65, the grandchild has taken increasing amounts of income starting with $2,575 and increasing every year to about $23,000. This is in addition to the value of the Roth IRA. Moreover, if the grandchild was particularly thrifty, he or she could have *further* reinvested the distribution in another interest earnings vehicle (NOT the Roth because that's not allowed) and had even more money to spend in retirement. It is important to note that these gains don't include the distributions taken over the years which can be spent or further invested, just not back into the Roth IRA.

Benefit of Gifting Appreciated Stock

Here is an example of how giving appreciated stock might benefit an heir, especially if the stock gifted grows substantially over time.

Apple stock sold in January of 1990 for $8.36 per share. In 2014, a single share of this stock is worth around $518 per share (at least at the time this book was printed).

Clearly, had you bought 1,000 shares at this price (even without stock splits, etc.) that 1,000 shares would represent a significant asset today. Even assuming a low-cost basis, you'd likely have a large capital gains bill if you sold the stock. However, by gifting a portion of the stock to a beneficiary in a lower tax bracket, the sale could be tax-free if the recipient is in a 15 percent tax bracket.

and—if the account is established in the parents' or the grandparents' name—some control over how the money is used by the beneficiary.[5] If the grandparent is the donor, we recommend this asset be established in the grandparent's name in case there is a divorce of the parents of the beneficiary. If the asset is in the name of the parent of the beneficiary and the parent divorces, the asset will be considered an asset of the marriage even if a grandparent contributed to it.

Establishing a Roth IRA

A Roth IRA is an excellent way to leave a tax-free cash legacy for your heirs. The main difference between a traditional IRA and a Roth IRA is that your contributions to a Roth IRA are not tax-deductible when initially invested in the fund. However, withdrawals are generally completely tax-free, and there are fewer restrictions on how and when the funds are withdrawn. Here are some other important points about a Roth IRA:

▶ You must be at least 59½ years old to withdraw the funds tax-free and have held the account at least five years.

▶ To fund a Roth IRA directly, your income must be less than $112,000 if you're single and $178,000 if you're married.

▶ Distributions from a Roth IRA don't increase your yearly adjusted gross income.

▶ Roth IRA assets can be passed along to your heirs.

▶ You are not required to begin withdrawing the funds upon reaching age 70½ (a big advantage in passing down tax-free assets to your heirs).

Again, these are just a few of the many advantages of a Roth IRA, but it's advisable to discuss this investment with a financial professional who's familiar with the specific rules for Roth IRA investing. The rules and implications can get quite complicated. This is particularly true if you're considering converting part of a traditional IRA to a Roth IRA because these transactions can be subject to substantial taxes if not done correctly.

Often, this advice involves spreading the conversion from a traditional IRA to a Roth IRA over a few years to avoid incurring a substantial tax liability if transferred all at once or the potential that this transfer might put you in a higher tax bracket. Here's an example of how this might work:

John and Mary Smith file their taxes jointly and had income in 2013 of $95,345. After a meeting with their financial advisor, they decide to convert $45,000 of their $500,000 IRA into a Roth IRA as part of a long-term retirement strategy. While their financial advisor told them that converting the full $45,000 of IRA assets to a Roth IRA was possible, he offered instead a money-solving strategy of converting a certain portion of the IRA each year until the full amount was reached. Not only would this strategy avoid a big one-time tax bill associated with the conversion (because IRS rules mandate payment of taxes on new income), but the slow transfer of funds avoids an overall increase in their yearly taxes due to a change in John and Mary's tax bracket.

Clearly, there are plenty of reasons to consider Roth IRAs as part of your retirement- and trust-planning considerations. But a Roth IRA really shines as a vehicle to provide a tax-free income for a grandchild or other heir. In fact, it's not that hard to construct a scenario in which a Roth IRA with an initial value of $200,000 could deliver more than $1 million of income for a beneficiary over their lifetime (See sidebar, page 109).

It is not possible to initially fund a Roth IRA for a grandchild to that $100,000 level except through conversion because cash gifting limits and other legal requirements still apply, including a requirement that the beneficiary has a job. Still, if you want to encourage your grandchild or your children to appreciate the value of saving and investment, you do have some options.

For example, it's perfectly legal to hire your own child to do chores around the house or perform duties for your business if you're self-employed. This employment allows a Roth IRA to be funded until your child or grandchild is gainfully employed outside the home.

Passing Down Appreciated Stock

Gifting appreciated stock is a good way to reduce the amount of capital-gains tax you pay. Currently, individuals can give up to $14,000 of appreciated stock to as many recipients as they wish without paying any gift taxes and for married individuals the amount goes up to $28,000 ($14,000 for each spouse).

The gift of appreciated stock does mean the beneficiary will be on the hook for the capital-gains tax based on the cost basis of the stock (how much the stock was worth on the day it was acquired). But in the case of a gift to children or grandchildren, this is a cost that may be avoided if the beneficiary's tax bracket (especially if the beneficiary is young or just starting a career) is in the 10 percent or 15 percent income tax bracket. If this were the case, then the sale would be tax-free.

Gifting Appreciated Stock to Charity

Gifting stock to a charitable organization also makes sense for anyone wishing to reduce their tax liability because both the donor and the charity avoid capital-gains taxes. Not only does this gift bring you a tax benefit, but the gift is ultimately more valuable to the charity. Again, it's best to work with a financial professional if you're considering this strategy because the various tax laws governing these transactions are complex. But to give you an idea of how this strategy plays out, here's an example.

Imagine that you'd like to gift $10,000 in appreciated stock to a favorite charity. Because you've owned the stock for more than a year, the gift is allowed under current tax law. When you bought the stock, it was worth $5,000 (the cost basis) and you know that even using the lowest capital-gains rate of 15 percent, you'd owe at least $750. However, if you donate the shares to your favorite charity, you get the full $10,000 tax deduction and you avoid the capital-gains tax as well.

Unfortunately, if this wise investment had gone south and instead of doubling in value it was worth only $500, you'd only be able to deduct this $500 from your taxes. A financial advisor might suggest selling the stock, making a cash gift of the proceeds ($500) to the charity, and then using the capital loss of $4,500 to offset any other capital gains.

Establishing a Life Insurance Trust

Buying a life insurance policy as the asset within an irrevocable trust is a commonly used strategy to reduce estate taxes. An irrevocable life insurance trust (ILIT) is a good way to set aside money to pay estate taxes because the owner (purchaser) of the policy no longer owns the asset once it is placed in a trust. The trustee manages the asset for the policy beneficiaries and facilitates passing the policy's value to the beneficiary, thus avoiding any applicable estate taxes.

Five-Star Tip: Make Cash Gifting a Win-Win

Gifting cash or stock to your heirs is a win-win strategy as long as you make sure that your generosity enables the success of your heirs.

The win for the benefactor is that gifting reduces potential tax liabilities. The win for the heir is that gifting enables the achievement of a goal such as home ownership, college, or even a creative dream such as improving an artistic skill.

However, you'll need to be deliberate about creating this win-win situation. These gifts can also disable by demotivating the recipient, so be careful.

One potential complication of using an ILIT is that the insured must transfer the policy to the trust at least three years before their death. It is often recommended that the ILIT purchase the policy at the outset so that the insured never actually owned the policy. While ILITs can be an excellent strategy for someone with a high-value estate (above $5.34 million for a single individual or $10.68 million for a married couple), for most of us any life insurance payout is considered part of an overall estate. Note that there are many other rules and consider-ations so you should discuss your options with an attorney.

Setting Up a Qualified Personal Residence Trust

A qualified personal residence trust (QPRT) is a tax-saving strategy associated with irre-vocable trusts. Essentially, the donor gifts ownership of the home or property and signs an agreement that allows the property donors to live in the home or property for a fixed amount of time. The strategy works best if the donor lives past the specified terms of the trust (the longer the term, the greater the tax advantage).

If properly structured, a QPRT will freeze the value of the donor's residence at the time of the trust's creation. At the end of the term, the residence transfers to the beneficiaries listed in the trust with the end result that the residence and its value are out of the donor's estate.

This is a very specialized gifting strategy so a qualified attorney must set up a QPRT under an irrevocable trust and care should be taken to not overestimate the life expectancy of the donor because the value in using this strategy is lost if the donor dies before the term ends. (Note: The trust only applies to the residence and not personal property such as furniture and art contained in the residence.) Also, the donor still has the right to use the residence in any way during the trust term, including renting it out. If the donor dies during the trust term, the value of the residence returns to the donor's estate.

Avoiding Inheritance Lottery Syndrome

When someone receives a great deal of money, a common response is to increase lifestyle to an unsustainable level. In many cases, the money disables the recipient because they often leave good jobs without understanding that the onetime event won't support the lifestyle they've developed and they eventually run out of money. Careful estate planning is the best way to manage how your heirs handle a sudden windfall of cash, stock, or other considerable assets. Depending on the size and complexity of your estate, what follows are some of the best strategies to ensure that your financial legacy enables your heirs to achieve their goals in life.

From Our Practice...
Enable Your Heirs with a Financial Legacy

No matter the amount, your financial legacy can either enable or disable your heirs. Few, if any, financial or estate planning experts would disagree with that statement. Whether the amount passed along is $50,000 or $5 million, you need to consider the heir's ability to put the inheritance to good use. Here's an example:

A client passed along a great deal of money to one of their children at the beginning of the 2008 financial crisis. Rather than using the money to build skills for future success or take advantage of investment opportunities in a down economy, the heir didn't work for two years and spent a huge portion of the money on frivolous activities. The client's heir reacted to the gift as if he had just won the lottery. I often call this the "lottery syndrome." Remember, over 70 percent of lottery winners end up broke because they are unable to manage the cash windfall.

A better strategy in this case would have been to set up some enabling requirements for the heir such as a stipulation that a portion of the money be used to put a down payment on an affordable house, expand an existing entrepreneurial business, start a new business, or fund a legacy for the heir's future family.

Sometimes this enablement is supported by expressed wishes in a will that a certain asset or a portion of an asset be used for a specific purpose: to encourage attending graduate school, to supplement a grandchild's educational fund, or to continue supporting a cause or charitable activity important to the donor. These are some specific suggestions you might include in your will and empower your trustee to be your advocate for these enabling uses of your financial legacy. And as noted previously, if you're concerned about how your financial legacy will be used, it is possible to stagger distributions over time.

Funding Your Children's or Grandchildren's Education

Although I have discussed savvy tax, estate, and trust planning strategies in this and earlier chapters, it bears repeating that funding the continuing education of your children and grandchildren is one of the best ways to ensure that your heirs use your financial legacy for a worthwhile purpose. Whether it's through funding a 529 plan or allowing only limited access to funds in an irrevocable trust, you can make your priorities clear to the next generation. (See illustration earlier in this chapter on 529 investments.)

Other Specific Purpose Designations

The trustee you appoint can actively encourage your heirs to use their inherited assets for practical purposes such as putting a down payment on a home, building their own retirement accounts, saving for future medical expenses, and paying for your grandchildren's daycare or early education.

If you've set up an irrevocable trust, your enforcement options can be creative and flexible. For example, you might require that your beneficiaries match your gift for a specific purpose (anything from travel, self-improvement, to buying a house) with funds of their own. It's not that you're intentionally being difficult or demanding unreasonable hurdles to deny access to your assets, it's just that you're trying to help your heirs make responsible financial and life choices.

Encouraging Charitable Giving

Americans are generally a charitable people. In fact, a recent National Philanthropic Trust report shows that the average household gives more than $2,200 to charity each year, a total of nearly $3 billion.[6]

The requirement can be as simple as expressing a wish to your trustee that a certain portion or amount of an estate be set aside as a donation to a particular religious institution or a nonprofit organization of their choice. You might even empower a trustee to make a regular distribution to a chosen charity from your trust to model your own commitment to giving back.

Giving Money to Achieve Goals

Not all enabling strategies involve traditional measures of success or achievement. Yes, education and charitable giving are responsible uses of money, but perhaps you'd like to support a beneficiary's long-term musical or sporting goal, i.e., joining the orchestra pit of a local theatre company, playing semiprofessional baseball, or hitting the big time on Broadway. These are all enabling inheritance strategies that a trustee can support and ensure that they are carried out.

Establishing Family Limited Partnerships

A Family Limited Partnership (FLP) is a limited business partnership controlled by family members. The general partners of the FLP bear 100 percent of the liability and control all of the management and investment decisions. Limited partners have limited liability and cannot participate in the management of the FLP.

The partnership itself is not a taxable entity, but the owners report their own partnership income and deductions on their individual personal tax returns. And more importantly, partners can gift or sell all or a portion of their interest in the FLP to their children and grandchildren. These interests can be gifted or sold to an irrevocable trust.

FLPs are often used to reduce a senior FLP member's estate tax by transferring their interest in the partnership to a family member. This transfer essentially establishes the donee as a limited partner, which limits their control over partnership investments and distributions; this action also provides further valuation tax breaks when the interest is transferred. Finally, FLPs protect the limited partner's other assets from creditors.

The tax law is a bit complicated, but it's important to understand the tax implications for both the share owners and their beneficiaries in an FLP transfer. First, once the shares are gifted, they are not recoverable by the gifting partner. Still, for a small business owner an FLP provides an excellent avenue to transfer a great deal of wealth to the next generation and reduce estate taxes. For example, a partner and his wife could potentially pass more than $10 million to an heir under an FLP and not pay any estate tax using their combined lifetime exemption amounts of $5.34 million each.

An FLP also provides legal cover for families that own housing or vacation properties against renter lawsuits, and partners enjoy serious tax savings when transferring the properties to the next generation.

Three Estate Planning Documents Everyone Needs

Regardless of your level of wealth, everyone should have at least three estate planning documents: a Will, a Healthcare Power of Attorney and a Financial Power of Attorney. These three documents allow you to specify what happens to your possessions and investments when you are gone, or to provide for dependent children and direct end-of-life care.

Making a Will is an important step in your financial management program. You can plan now for the orderly transfer of your property to save your heirs time and money. You decide to whom, when, and in what amounts your assets should go. You select your executor or personal representative, the one who is responsible for the disposition of the estate. Without a Will your estate must be distributed according to the intestate laws of the state where you reside, the provisions of which are often general and inflexible. The law will say who will administer your estate, among whom, and how it shall be divided. Without a Will you lose the privilege of naming a guardian for your minor children. This is vital, particularly if your spouse should not survive you. If you leave no immediate family, failure to leave a will may result in your property going to persons in whom you have no particular interest.

A Healthcare Power of Attorney, also called a Healthcare Proxy or a Durable Power of Attorney for Healthcare, helps protect your end-of-life wishes. It is a document that appoints a trusted individual to make decisions regarding your medical care, and it becomes effective when you can no longer communicate effectively or coherently with others.

A Financial Durable Power of Attorney can give you the peace of mind that should you become unable to make important choices for yourself that affect you, your family, and/or your finances, then you—not a court—would choose who would make those important choices.

What's Next and Wrap Up

The next chapter of this book, *Confront Life's Challenges with a Positive Attitude*, is all about building the financial and emotional strength you need if your personal life expectations—love, marriage, family, and growing old with your chosen partner for life—don't pan out as planned. This chapter tackles the unexpected detours the challenges bring and offers essential short- and long-term strategies to help you weather these personal and financial storms.

Here's a recap of the key information presented in this chapter:

▶ Setting up a trust can offer significant tax savings for you and your beneficiaries.

▶ Choose a trustee who won't allow personal opinions, pre-existing loyalties, and biases to cloud decisions. Choose someone you trust completely.

▶ You lose control of any asset or property placed in an irrevocable trust.

▶ You can make changes in revocable trust asset allocations during your life.

▶ Assets held in revocable trusts are not considered part of the donor's probate estate. This means lower fees and less time-consuming procedural hurdles.

▶ Cash gifting ultimately reduces the potential tax liability associated with the estate you pass along to your heirs.

▶ A single individual can give up to $14,000 per year to as many individuals as they wish while a married couple can give up to $28,000 to as many individuals as they wish per year.

▶ Income tax on the gift is paid by the recipient when sold on the original cost basis of the gift asset.

▶ As long as 529 gifts are used to pay for qualified educational expenses, the withdrawals are completely tax-free.

▶ A Roth IRA is an excellent way to leave a tax-free cash legacy with fewer restrictions on how and when funds are withdrawn. Capital gains, dividends and interest activity that occur within the fund are also passed along tax-free.

▶ Individuals can gift up to $14,000 of appreciated stock to as many recipients as they wish without paying any gift taxes.

▶ Gifting appreciated stock to charitable organizations reduces the tax liability of the donor and allows the charity to use the full value of the appreciated stock.

▶ Setting up an irrevocable life insurance trust is a good way to set aside money to pay estate taxes for heirs because the insured no longer owns the asset once it is placed in a trust.

▶ A qualified personal residence trust is a tax-saving strategy that allows the donor to gift ownership of the property and live in the residence for a fixed amount of time.

▶ Motivate and enable your heirs to achieve their goals and succeed in life by specifically attaching an intended use to an asset such as attending graduate school, supplementing a grandchild's educational fund, or encouraging the support of charitable causes.

▶ Setting up a family limited partnership allows partners in a property or business to gift a portion of their interest in the FLP to their children and grandchildren and realize great estate tax savings.

CHAPTER 9

Confront Life's Challenges with a Positive Attitude

In This Chapter

▶ Survive the Pitfalls of Divorce

▶ Deal with the Death of a Spouse

▶ Retire and Live on Your Own

No matter how much we try, sometimes our financial and personal lives don't go as planned. We fall in and out of love; we marry and divorce; we dream about growing old with our soul mate only to watch them die too soon. It's the same dance humans have done with life's realities for thousands of years. Still, as well-grounded adults we do our best to celebrate the joy, accept the pain and sorrow, and find positive meaning in life's unexpected and even unwelcome events.

This chapter is about what to do when your personal life expectations—love, marriage, family, and growing old with your chosen partner for life—don't pan out as planned. This chapter tackles both the financial and emotional consequences of such unexpected detours and offers essential short- and long-term financial strategies specifically targeted to facing these challenges.

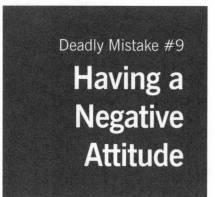

Deadly Mistake #9

Having a Negative Attitude

The first section of the chapter provides a general overview of these difficulties and offers guidance on persevering through the emotional and financial effects of each. The final section offers essential guidelines for getting your life back on track after a divorce, losing a spouse, or any other circumstance that might result in retiring on your own.

The Value of Marriage

Despite radically changed ideas about who, when, and how we marry, the marriage contract is still the cultural glue that binds all humans and their cultures and communities together. Still, to put the current state of marriage in context, here are some interesting statistics to consider.

A July 2013 study by Bowling Green University's National Center for Family and Marriage Research (NCFMR) found the marriage rate among women to be at its lowest point in nearly 100 years—31.1 percent—compared to 92.3 percent in 1920. The same NCFMR study also found that the average first marriage age is 27 years old—also at its highest point in 97 years—and that 15 percent of women are now divorced, as compared to a rate of 1 percent in 1920.[1]

Despite these marriage rate statistics, the fact remains that we are predisposed to the idea of marriage by tradition, and at a more fundamental level, by our evolutionary history. While millions of couples do skip the legal entanglements of a formal marriage contract to live together, these arrangements are often just a compatibility test on the road to marriage.

I note these cultural and practical forces that favor marriage only to highlight an important financial aspect about marriage: married individuals still get preferential tax breaks at both the federal and state level. This fact alone can significantly affect your current and long-term financial options and even affect how and when you can retire. So at least from a financial planning point of view, marriage is a good deal, and it's an especially good deal if you get married and stay married.

Emotional and Financial Pitfalls of Divorce

It's hard to find an accurate statistical picture of how many marriages end in divorce. For example, a 2011 Centers for Disease Control study showed that the number of divorces as a percentage of the U.S. population has remained pretty much the same (around 4% per 1,000 citizens) since 2000; the average percentage in 2011 was 3.6 percent per 1,000 citizens.[2] How these statistics relate to the U.S. divorce rate over time is unclear, but the generally reported statistic (especially in the media) is that 50 percent of first marriages end in divorce, 67 percent of second marriages don't work out, and an astounding 73 percent of third marriages fail.[3]

Five-Star Tip: Avoid Divorce

I always dispense the same advice to clients seeking financial guidance about divorce: if you think your marriage is failing, try to work it out. There are no winners in a divorce!

Suffice it to say, whatever the real numbers are, divorce is responsible for a tremendous amount of financial and emotional damage starting with the partners involved and extending to their children and their families. That's why I always dispense the same advice to clients seeking financial guidance about divorce: if you think your marriage is failing, try to work it out. There are no winners in a divorce!

Of course, sometimes it's just not possible to save a marriage, and all I can do is offer these clients practical financial advice so that they make the best decisions possible in the transition to being single again and, as inevitably happens, when they prepare to marry again.

Why people divorce is a complex question I won't even attempt to cover, but the most often stated reasons are worth noting: busy careers and lives, too much focus on the children and not on each other, and infidelity.

My advice, whether the client is middle-aged or recently retired, is to take a step back from the situation and take a fresh look at your spouse without the baggage of past resentments and arguments and try to fall in love again. I also suggest seeking out professional counseling before making a final divorce decision while emphasizing the "no winners" mantra.

If saving the marriage is not possible, then the next best option is to limit the emotional and financial damage as much as possible. This advice includes strategies to ensure that both parties have every opportunity to be honest, ethical, and civil in their dealings with each other.

On a practical level, I help these clients think through the ways the divorce will affect their lives. I include in this checklist the relationships they have with their children and relatives. Then, there are the important financial consequences of divorce, including future educational expenses for children, paying household bills on one income, and ensuring adequate healthcare coverage for each individual.

Social Security Considerations

The rules for collecting Social Security benefits when you're divorced are not that complex, but as always you'll need to pay attention to the exceptions and considerations clauses. But in general, here are the rules for divorced individuals from the Social Security Administration:

- ▶ If you are divorced, you can receive benefits based on your ex-spouse's benefits record (even if they have remarried) if:
  - your marriage lasted 10 years or longer
  - you are unmarried
  - you are age 62 or older
  - your ex-spouse is entitled to Social Security retirement or disability benefits and
  - the benefit you are entitled to receive based on your own work record is less than the benefit you would receive based on your ex-spouse's work record.

- ▶ A divorced spouse's benefit is equal to one-half of your ex-spouse's full retirement amount (or disability benefit) if you start receiving benefits at your full retirement age.

- ▶ If you claim the benefit between age 62 and your full retirement age, the benefit amount will be permanently reduced by a percentage based on the number of months up to your full retirement age.

▶ If you remarry, you generally cannot collect benefits on your former spouse's record unless your later marriage ends (whether by death, divorce or annulment).

▶ The amount of benefits you get has no effect on the amount of benefits your ex-spouse or their current spouse may receive.

▶ If your ex-spouse is deceased, there are some specific guidelines from the Social Security Administration:

  • If you are divorced and your former spouse dies, you could get the same benefits as a widow or widower provided that your marriage lasted 10 years or more.

  • If you remarry after you reach age 60 (age 50 if disabled), the remarriage will not affect your eligibility for survivor's benefits.

  • Benefits paid to you as a surviving divorced spouse won't affect the benefit rates for other survivors claiming benefits on your former spouse's work record.

The Death of a Spouse

Some statistics suggest that nearly 14 percent of all Americans between the ages of 55 and 64 are currently widowed. Other sources suggest that more than 40 percent of women over age 65 are widows.[4] But if you're trying to gauge the chances of losing your spouse between 55 and 80 years of age, take a look at Figures 9.1 and 9.2 from a 2010 study conducted by the Social Security Administration that examined income levels of older Americans. Here's what the study revealed:

▶ between the ages of 55 and 61, 2.1 percent of men were widowed

▶ between the ages of 62 and 69, the percentage of widowed men rose to 4.6 percent

▶ between the ages of 70 and 74, the percentage of widowed men rose only slightly to 7.8 percent

Percentage of Widowed Men
(ages 55-over 80)

	Age 55-61	Age 62-69	Age 70-74	Age 75-79	Over 80 yrs.
70%					
50%					
30%					
10%					
2%					

Figure 9.1

▶ between the ages of 75 and 79, the widowed men percentage doubled to 15.1 percent and peaked at 28.8 percent for men older than 80.

Women, however, appear to be more likely to lose their spouses in their middle and later years. According to the study, the widowed status of women and men is similar in the early years of retirement age, although it is slightly higher for women. But the widowed status increases greatly beginning at age 65:

▶ between the ages of 62 and 69, 19.3 percent of women were widowed

▶ between the ages of 75 and 79, 47.3 percent of women were widowed

▶ and for women over the age of 80, nearly 67 percent of women were widowed.[5]

While these statistics are revealing and interesting in their own way, I offer them more as a reality check. As unfortunate as it is, many of us will lose spouses—especially women—so thinking through and planning for the possibility of losing a spouse just makes sense.

As you'll see in my guidelines that follow, the passing of a spouse means that you're responsible for attending to many tasks—some mundane and practical

Percentage of Widowed Women
(ages 55-over 80)

	Age 55-61	Age 62-69	Age 70-74	Age 75-79	Over 80 yrs.
70%					
50%					
30%					
10%					
2%					

Figure 9.2

and others critically important to your financial security.

The practical tasks include a range of activities from obtaining a death certificate to gathering up financial records and updating the ownership status for credit and checking accounts to ensuring that all household bills are paid. In addition, you'll need to make more complex and nuanced decisions regarding investment and retirement accounts, and these require the advice of a financial or legal advisor. It's all important and it's covered in my guidelines.

Retiring and Living on Your Own

While it would not be advisable to attach a great deal of statistical meaning to these numbers, I do think they help paint a picture of the general marital landscape I'm addressing in this chapter. Women generally outlive men. Most of us marry at some point in our lives. Divorce is a significant factor in the lives of many Americans.

But despite any conclusions we might draw from these statistics, the fact is most of us assume that these statistics will never have anything to do with our own lives, i.e., the classic "that will never happen to me" response. It's fine to think that, but as a financial advisor for the past 30 years, I'd suggest it's a good idea to be prepared just in case.

The following guidelines offer the structural underpinnings for the many decisions that you'll have to make due to a divorce, death of a spouse, or other circumstance that ends with the same result: you're single again.

1. Take Some Time Off to Avoid Emotion-Driven Decisions

Whether you've gone through a divorce or the death of a spouse, it's important to avoid making emotion-driven decisions. Take some time to recover emotionally so that you can make clearheaded decisions. In the meantime, focus on practical matters including these:

▶ Gather up all financial records including insurance policies and other legal and benefit documents.

▶ Make sure all of your recurring bills (including mortgage, credit card, and utility) are paid while you update the account status.

▶ Change the title on your home.

▶ Check on your continuing health coverage.

These and all of the other details of transitioning to single status should be part of a master list of activities you create and methodically work through. Some of the items on your list might require the help of someone with specific expertise such as a lawyer or financial expert. Other items might require the help of a trusted friend or family member. Here are some other important items that should be on your list:

▶ **Death Certificate.** You'll need an original formal death certificate to complete many of the financial and property transfer activities required after the death of a spouse. It's a good idea to get perhaps a dozen copies of this document because an original copy is often needed for some transactions.

▶ **Insurance Policies.** You'll need to determine benefits and how and when these will be paid.

▶ **Other Official Certificates.** You're likely to need these documents at some point in the transition process if your spouse has died:
- marriage certificate
- birth certificates for dependent children
- certificate of discharge from the military
- complete list of all property.

▶ **Copy of Your Will.** This original copy is often in a safe deposit box, but you may also have a copy in the financial records you keep at home.

▶ **Access to Safe Deposit Box.** If possible, it's a good idea to take out important documents before your spouse's death because some states seal the boxes after a death, even if the box is registered in the name of both spouses.

▶ **Life Insurance Benefits.** If you are listed as the beneficiary, you should get the cash in either a lump sum or fixed payments. All of this may take several weeks. If your spouse has named you as the only beneficiary, contact your insurance company or lawyer to name another beneficiary as soon as possible.

▶ **Social Security Benefits.** You are eligible for a $255 death payment for funeral expenses, and depending on your age or if you have dependent children, you might be eligible for survivor's benefits (see sidebar).

▶ **Employee Benefits.** If your spouse had company life insurance, a 401(k) plan, or any other company benefits, contact the human resources manager at your spouse's company. Depending on the size of the company, you might be eligible to continue health insurance under your spouse's policy.

▶ **Veteran's Benefits.** If your spouse served in the military, you might be eligible for burial expenses or other expenses such as a headstone or a free burial in a national cemetery. Contact the Veterans Affairs Department to determine your eligibility.

▶ **Other Benefits.** If your spouse belonged to a credit union, a labor union, the American Legion, or another national organization, you might be eligible for certain benefits afforded to members.

Beyond these items on your checklist, you should contact your financial and/or legal advisor to notify them of your situation. If any of the items on your long to-do list are too complex or emotionally draining, the best financial planning firms will do most, if not all, of the work for you, including contacting banks and changing your various brokerage accounts.

The tax issues facing someone who has lost a spouse or is going through a divorce can be quite complex and are best handled by a professional financial, tax, or legal expert. For example, if your spouse dies you're required to file an estate tax return within nine months if the assets exceed the $5.34 million threshold for estate taxes. If this is the case, you'll need to file a form 706 with the Internal Revenue Service to receive a $5.34 million federal estate exemption for your deceased spouse. The requirements vary between states and some may also impose an estate tax or inheritance tax. As with all potentially complex legal decisions, discuss these decisions with a qualified legal or tax professional.

As noted in the last chapter, these taxes can be as high as 40 percent so an estate of this size needs professional management. If your spouse leaves the entire estate to you, then you can avoid estate tax under a tax code provision called the unlimited marital deduction.

In addition, you're required to file federal and state income tax for the income that your spouse earned up to the time of death. And remember, you can file jointly as long as you don't remarry prior to the end of the year that your spouse died. (Note: If you have a child still at home when your spouse dies, you can file jointly for two additional years beyond your spouse's death.)

Finally, if your residence or stock portfolio account has had a large gain over a number of years, you reap substantial tax advantages using what is known as a "step up in basis" allowance. In practice, this means that if you originally paid $50,000 for your house and it is now worth $1 million, you could claim its value as being 50 percent of its original value plus 50 percent of its current value: a resulting value of $525,000.

As a final word of caution, don't wait to take action on the applicable steps I've outlined here. Some actions such as getting a death certificate are required and unavoidable while others such as updating credit card information or dealing with estate or various tax implications may not seem like immediate concerns. Unfortunately, waiting can have short- and long-term consequences including additional financial burdens, legal ramifications, and even creditworthiness if your bills are not paid on time.

2. Reassess and Recalibrate Your Life

Whether your single status is the result of a divorce or death of a spouse, you should take six months to a year to consider your options before making major decisions including whether to sell your home. If you can't afford to keep your home, it's obviously better to sell it than to put yourself in a financial bind trying to keep it. I've had clients who received a large divorce settlement only to squander it away trying to maintain their pre-divorce lifestyle.

Depending on your age and interests, being single again might present an opportunity to re-engage with a career or hobby that you love. Often, being single again is a time to re-invent your life, and that can mean any-

Social Security Rules for the Widowed

Here are the official rules for widowed individuals from the Social Security Administration, assuming your spouse was eligible for benefits. You can:

- receive 100% of your spouse's benefit amount when you reach full retirement age.

- receive 71% to 99% of your spouse's basic benefit amount if you receive benefits before your full retirement age.

- remarry after you reach age 60 (age 50 if disabled) without your remarriage affecting your eligibility for survivor's benefits.

thing from going back to school to getting a new or first college degree or taking painting classes.

3. Look for Love, Just Look Before You Leap

As the statistics I presented earlier indicate, there's a good chance that many of us will date and perhaps remarry. If you've lost your spouse, the issues you'll face with family and friends are different from those of someone who divorced. Still, no matter your situation, seek out the advice of trusted friends or others you believe can offer objective advice about someone you're serious about. Family members, especially in the case of divorce, are not reliable sounding boards.

I also advise my clients to be very cautious about revealing too much financial information, especially if their financial assets are significant. Unfortunately, it's not unusual for predators to take advantage of the fragile emotional state of someone who's lost a spouse or divorced.

As I noted, those navigating the family and financial issues of divorce have a particularly difficult time, especially if the divorce was not amicable. The best advice I can offer these clients is that they learn the four Cs: counseling, communicating, compromising, and collaborating. It's a difficult time—the financial issues aside—so the divorcing parties should seek some type of professional help to ensure that they will continue to communicate. Then use the counseling and communication to compromise and collaborate on the best solution for themselves, their children, and the extended family. Finally, it's not a bad idea to check the credit history (and in some cases, criminal history) of someone you intend to marry. If you've got a substantial amount of money then you can't be too careful.

If you do remarry, here are some top recommendations:

▶ Keep your finances separate. This prevents future money and spending arguments, and if you co-mingle your assets, this blending cannot be undone. Considering the failure rate of second marriages, this just doesn't seem like a good idea.

▶ Write a new will. Engage an attorney and produce a new will that addresses your new situation and beneficiary priorities.

▶ Revisit trust arrangements. Make sure your assets are protected and go to the beneficiary of your choice, e.g., directly to your children.

4. Understand Your Investments to Maximize Your Return and Minimize Your Risk

Whether you've lost a spouse, divorced, or been single for all of your life, it's essential that you invest for the future and fund your retirement. I've outlined a great many strategies in this book from budgeting to taxes that will ensure you have a steady cash flow in retirement.

> **The Four Cs**
>
> The best advice for divorcing couples is to look for solutions by following the four Cs:
>
> 1. counseling
>
> 2. communicating
>
> 3. compromising
>
> 4. collaborating.

Just because you're on your own again doesn't mean the basic rules for sustainable finances have changed. You'll still have to budget and maintain enough asset liquidity to ensure you can pay your bills and live the life you want. It might be difficult to change your spending habits, but remember you have less money to pay the same amount of expenses. And don't forget, if you've lost your spouse, in some cases you also lose their Social Security benefits.

The financial calculations for divorce are different from those of a widow. For example, if you are negotiating an alimony payment, make sure you include the cost of inflation in the settlement. As I pointed out earlier in this book, a payment of $1,000 today must be $1,040 next year (assuming 4% inflation) just to keep valuation the same. Life insurance for the spouse responsible for support must also be calibrated to include inflation cost over time. You'll also need to be as detailed as possible about potential costs for education, including clothes, tuition, books, etc.

5. Actively Manage Your Income and Cash Flow by Making a Budget and Following It

This book (and its associated website, www.onlyretireonce.com) offers an excellent budgeting tool that will be helpful as you adjust to a single lifestyle. Remember, you'll have perhaps 50 percent of your former income – to pay the same expenses. I often tell my clients that they will need 70 to 80 percent of their former income to live as a single person whether they are divorced or widowed. These extra expenses include everything from greater healthcare coverage costs to shuttling between homes and states to see children to the cost of dating.

And here's an interesting conundrum for both widowers and divorcees. If you were married more than 10 years and remarry before you're 60 you won't have access to your spouse's Social Security payment. (Download a retirement app for Android and iPhone at www.onlyretireonce.com)

6. Plan for Longevity

Finally, as I have repeated throughout this book you must plan for longevity whether you lose your spouse through death or divorce or live your entire life as a single person. The same challenge of paying for long-term care persists no matter your marital status. In fact, this need might even be greater because you won't have your spouse's help in your later years.

From Our Practice...

Advice for the Divorced or Widowed

As I noted in this chapter, the actual percentage of divorced or widowed Americans is a difficult statistic to pin down. Still, it's safe to assume that at any given moment millions of people are making important decisions based on their marital status, and these decisions directly affect their financial status. Maybe that's why financial planning experts sometimes serve double duty as the client's money and life/relationship manager.

While I might relay some instructive stories from my own client experiences, perhaps a list of recommendations based on these experiences would be more useful and instructive. So to that end, here are some key recommendations for any widowed or divorced individual:

- If an old high school flame suddenly gets in touch after the death of a spouse or a divorce, be careful. Remember, it's easy for potential predators to determine if they can exploit you or your spouse's success.

- Take your time and choose new partners wisely. If in doubt about a potential partner's claims, don't be afraid to verify what they say. If the potential partner is insulted, then seriously reconsider the relationship. The bottom line: if someone says they have millions and you have doubts, don't be afraid to say, "show me."

- Although it goes without saying, never give anyone you're dating financial information or access to your asset accounts.

- In most cases, it makes sense to create some type of prenuptial agreement when you remarry.

- If you remarry, don't mix assets. Remember, the failure rate for second marriages is higher than for first marriages and the failure rate for third marriages is higher than both first and second marriages.

- Regularly re-evaluate your trust documents and will to ensure your assets stay with the beneficiaries you intend.

What's Next and Wrap Up

This chapter touched on ways to deal with the personal and financial consequences of your personal life expectations—love, marriage, family, and growing old with your chosen partner for life—not going as planned. The appendix offers practical tools to help you make the right budget and financial planning decisions no matter the hand that life deals you.

Here's a recap of the key information presented in this chapter:

▶ Despite changed societal attitudes and ideas about marriage, there are clear emotional, cultural, and financial reasons to marry and stay married.

▶ The key guidelines to living on your own after divorce or the death of a spouse include the following:

- Avoid emotion-driven decisions by taking some time off.

- Sort out your options while reassessing and recalibrating your life.

- Look before you leap when re-engaging with your life.

- Maximize investment returns and minimize risk.

- Carefully manage your cash flow.

- Plan for longevity by continuing to watch your budget.

- Regularly re-evaluate your trust documents and will to ensure your assets stay with the beneficiaries you intend.

CHAPTER 10

Plan for Your Retirement

In This Chapter

▶ Planning the Life You Want

▶ Taking the Next Steps

▶ Avoiding the Nine Deadly Planning Sins

Without question, the life we imagine for ourselves after retirement is vastly different from what our parents and grandparents could even begin to imagine.

Part of the reason previous generations found it necessary to lower their expectations was due to the vagaries of history and constraining, even debilitating, economic conditions at the time, i.e., the Great Depression and World War II. The 10,000 baby boomers currently retiring every day[1] have faced no such angst-producing hardships and challenges. In fact, a vast number of boomers and successive generations of Americans have had an easy ride over the last 40 to 60 years. So they now expect their retirement years to be no different than their pre-retirement experience of living in large, comfortable homes, driving late-model cars, traveling, and dining freely in fine restaurants.

Unfortunately, this latest group of American retirees have spent freely (often on credit) and saved little, apparently hoping that the future would take care of itself. But hope is not much of a planning tool.

Fortunately, all is not lost, especially for those willing to take action sooner rather than later. And even if it is getting late in the game, strategies are available (many noted in this book) that maximize asset value and make the most of every dollar spent.

The retirement planning strategies in this book offer help and hope to anyone willing to honestly face their retirement situation, including those planning retirement in 20 years as well as those planning retirement in five years. After all, the baseline questions are the same and focus first on describing the life you want and second on devising a financial strategy that will deliver the cash flow needed to fund that retirement vision. Of course, as I demonstrated in the book, every retirement plan must be tempered with the hard reality of choice. Sometimes cash flow and dreams are impossible to reconcile so we're forced to make hard choices between two equally important retirement priorities. Other times, we're forced to admit that our retirement vision will never be affordable.

Still, as disappointing as it might be to discover long-held retirement dreams are not immediately affordable (and perhaps will never be), this book provides a way to proactively make these choices. And for many not accustomed to such planning, the clarity of choice between well thought-out options will be a refreshing and liberating approach for the reader.

Taking the Next Steps

We've all heard the advice that every journey begins with the first step. The same strategy works just fine for retirement planning. So what are the first steps you should take? Here's a list to get you started:

1. Carefully assess your current financial situation.

This part is easy. The budgeting documents provided in the appendix and on the associated website (www.onlyretireonce.com) can serve as a template to assess your current financial situation and monitor your progress toward meeting your retirement goals.

2. *Find a financial planning professional you trust.*

This step may not be necessary for someone in their 30s or even early 40s, but you shouldn't wait much longer. As I've demonstrated numerous times in this book, financial professionals often make the difference in achieving your financial goals.

3. *Use every resource to become a savvy retirement planner.*

Clearly, this book is a solid resource to begin this part of your retirement planning journey, but take advantage of the thousands of available resources that will help you plan for and live out your retirement vision. Whether it's using government-sponsored websites to estimate your potential Social Security benefits (www.SSA.gov), plan for Medicare benefits (www.medicare. gov), or obtain healthcare benefit information (www.healthcare.gov), take time to research these and the thousands of articles, research reports, and other books on the topic of retirement planning.

4. *Be consistent.*

Once you have a retirement plan and thoroughly understand what you need to do to meet your retirement goals, work with your financial advisor to update your plan based on your own financial situation as well as economic and policy changes that might affect your plan.

Avoiding the Nine Deadly Sins of Retirement Savings

No set of rules and guidelines will ensure that you won't commit the most heartbreaking and stressful sin of retirement planning—running out of money at the end of your life. This book provides a broad-brush tour of the many considerations that should be part of any comprehensive retirement plan, but the devil is in the details. That's why it's so important to get help from a professional to make sure you've left nothing to chance. As I have consistently pointed out in this book, sometimes it's the overlooked detail that determines the quality of your life when you retire. Still, if you consistently avoid these nine sins of retirement saving, you'll have a better chance than most to retire and live the life you've always planned to live.

1. Don't Outlive Your Savings by Underestimating How Long You'll Live

▶ Think of retirement planning like building a house. Start with the big picture before worrying about the details.

▶ Remember, you have a very good chance of living well into your 90s. Be prepared!

▶ Make sure your retirement assets are secure; monitor their performance and seek out reliable advice.

▶ Construct a retirement plan you can live with and afford.

▶ Plan carefully and don't take hasty action.

▶ Don't be surprised by the high cost of retirement. Remember, every day is a Saturday.

2. Avoid Financial Surprises by Planning Ahead

▶ Plan for everything to cost more than you anticipate.

▶ Retire with as little debt as possible.

▶ If possible, retire debt- and mortgage-free.

▶ Be very cautious about using your home equity. If you do use it, pay it off as quickly as possible.

▶ Have a good attitude by accepting that life is full of surprises.

▶ Make sure that everything you do for your heirs enables their potential success in life.

▶ Healthcare WILL BE more expensive than you think.

▶ Nobody wins in a divorce. Stay married if possible and avoid divorce.

3. Create a Realistic Budget

▶ Embrace the liberating, not limiting, experience of a realistic retirement budget.

▶ Respect the power of inflation to reduce the value of your portfolio.

▶ Plan to spend more than you might ever imagine.

▶ Keep a substantial emergency fund for both major and minor home disasters.

▶ Always be a smart consumer, and never waste your assets.

4. *Use Smart Asset Management to Keep a Steady Cash Flow*

▶ Avoid adjustable rate mortgages even if the rates are substantially lower than fixed rate loans.

▶ Create continuing asset value by taking reasonable and appropriate investment risks.

▶ Avoid loaning money to friends, even when you think you can afford it.

▶ Create a retirement income plan strategy that taps into your retirement and nonretirement accounts to maximize long-term viability of resources.

▶ Retire in a bull market (a market trending up) if at all possible.

5. *Maximize Social Security Benefits*

▶ Retire when the annual cost of living adjustments are at a peak.

▶ Delay collecting Social Security benefits for as long as possible.

▶ Use a spousal-benefit strategy if appropriate for your situation.

▶ Use a file-and-suspend strategy to add extra benefits to your cash flow.

▶ Understand and use Social Security rules and requirements to ensure you claim all of the benefits for you, your family, your dependents, and your former spouse(s).

6. *Don't Underestimate Healthcare Costs*

▶ Do due diligence if you plan to move to another state to ensure that healthcare coverage and services are the same.

▶ Don't assume assisted-living and nursing home costs are the same between all of the states. While the average cost of nursing home care is $90,520 a year, similar services are $134,320 in New York and $250,775 a year in Alaska.

7. *Don't Overpay Your Tax Liability*

▶ Create a smart income plan that reduces your annual tax burden while preserving assets for your heirs.

▶ Gift appreciated stock to charities to ensure the best tax break for you and the greatest asset value for the charity.

▶ Always take dividends as cash for income.

▶ Directly gift low cost basis stock to your children or grandchildren in lower tax brackets and reduce your taxable income.

8. *Make Sure Your Estate Plan Enables Your Heirs*

▶ Choose a trustee who won't allow personal opinions, pre-existing loyalties, and biases to cloud the decisions.

▶ Use revocable and irrevocable trusts to lower taxes and fees; avoid legal and procedural hurdles that delay the transfer of your financial legacy to your heirs.

▶ Use cash gifting to reduce potential tax liabilities.

▶ Use 529 gifts to pay qualified educational expenses, and withdrawals are completely tax-free.

▶ Consider a Roth IRA as a way to leave a tax-free cash legacy for your heirs.

▶ Use an irrevocable life insurance trust to set aside money to pay estate taxes for heirs.

▶ Consider the use of a qualified personal residence trust to gift property ownership.

▶ Motivate and enable your heirs by specifying how your financial legacy will be used.

▶ Use a family limited partnership to gift a portion of a business to children and grandchildren to realize an estate tax savings.

9. *Always Be Positive in the Face of Life's Challenges*

▶ If possible, avoid divorce. No one wins.

▶ Remember the guidelines to living life after a divorce or death of a spouse.

▶ Take some time and avoid emotion-driven decisions.

▶ Reassess and recalibrate your life.

▶ Look before you leap into relationships.

▶ Make smart financial decisions.

▶ Maximize investment returns and minimize risk.

▶ Carefully manage your cash flow.

▶ Plan for longevity, and watch your budget.

Retirement Planning: My Bottom-Line Advice

Retirement planning is a complicated and often confusing assignment for anyone to take on, so hire an expert to help you.

Sure, you can find answers to most of your specific questions—how to sign up for Social Security benefits or recommended ways to save on taxes—by tapping into the vast reserve of information on the Internet and in print. But unless this information is part of a goal-oriented retirement plan that's also been skillfully integrated with a financial plan designed to maximize the income potential of your assets over time, then all of that information has little real value.

I look at it this way. No amount of research and study would make me confident enough to conduct my own brain surgery—even if that were possible. Retirement planning isn't brain surgery, but the two do-it-yourself options are similar in this way: even the smallest mistake (whether it's due to surgical precision or paying more taxes than necessary) has the potential to affect the quality and even quantity of the rest of your life. With such high stakes, is retirement planning really a DIY project you want to take on?

Roy Williams

This appendix offers supplemental information intended to promote understanding and application of the concepts presented in this book. A great deal of the information presented here can also be found on this book's associated website (www.onlyretireonce.com).

Additional reference information is duplicated from publicly available websites or generated by the staff of Prestige Wealth Management specifically for this book. This appendix includes the following content:

Worksheets and Checklists

▶ Personal Finance Balance Sheet

▶ Personal Finance Income and Expense Sheet

▶ Social Security Benefits Checklist

Informational Tables

▶ 2014 Medicare Costs at a Glance

Personal Finance Balance Sheet

ASSETS

Personal Income-Producing Assets

	Self	Spouse	Joint - ROS*
Brokerage Account (Nonqualified) Assets			
Retirement Account (Qualified) Assets			
Pension/Deferred Compensation			
Certificates of Deposit (CDs)			
Personal Loans Owed to You			
Insurance Cash Values			
Trust Account Assets			
Real Estate (Rental Property)			
Farm Land			
Miscellaneous			

Personal Nonincome-Producing Assets

	Self	Spouse	Joint - ROS*
Real Estate (Primary Residence)			
Real Estate (Second Home)			
Vacation Homes (Nonrental)			
Raw Land			
Cash/Checking and Savings Accounts			
Automobiles/RVs			
Boats			
Airplanes			
Antiques			
Coins/Collectibles			
Paintings/Artwork			
Jewelry			
Livestock			
Miscellaneous			

Business Assets

	Business
Building	
Equipment	
Accounts Receivable	
Intangibles	
Loans Owed to Your Business	
Miscellaneous	

*Right of Survivorship

LIABILITIES

	Self	Spouse	Joint - ROS *

Short-Term Liabilities

Liability	Self	Spouse	Joint - ROS
Credit Card Balances			
Unpaid Real Estate Taxes			
Unpaid Income Taxes			
Miscellaneous			

Long-Term Liabilities

Liability	Self	Spouse	Joint - ROS
Home Mortgage			
Automobiles/RVs/Boat Loans			
HELOC			
Unsecured Loans			
Secured Loans			
401(k) Loan			
College/Student Loans (for children/grandchildren)			
Miscellaneous			

Business Liabilities

Liability	
Loans Your Business Owes	
Accounts Payable	
Miscellaneous	

TOTAL ASSETS (page 1) $_____

LESS TOTAL LIABILITIES (page 2)   ($_____)

NET WORTH: $_____

*Right of Survivorship

Monthly Income Sources

1. Employment	Self	Spouse
Gross Salary		
Bonuses, Incentive Pay, etc.		
Unemployment Benefits		
Pension Benefits		
Miscellaneous		

2. Interest and Dividends	Self	Spouse
Checking and Savings Account Interest		
Investment Dividends and Interest		

3. Other Income		
Retirement Account Distributions**		
Beneficiary IRA Distributions		
Annuities (annuitized or immediate)		
Social Security Benefits		
Consulting Income		
Trust-Fund Income		
Alimony/Child Support		
Rental Property Income		
Mortgage Payments (incoming)		
Parental/Relative Gifts (ongoing)		
Royalties		
Miscellaneous		
Total Gross Income		

4. Income Taxes	Self	Spouse	Business
Federal Income Taxes			
State Income Taxes (if applicable)			
Local Income Taxes (if applicable)			
Social Security Taxes (if applicable)			
Payroll Taxes (if applicable)			

NET INCOME			

**RMDs from traditional IRAs must begin at age 70-1/2, but
   Roth IRAs require no distributions.

Monthly Fixed Expenses

Items in GREY are expenses that are likely to increase in retirement.

1. Mortgage and Home/Condo Expenses	1st Home	2nd Home	Business
Monthly Mortgage (principal and interest)			
Property Taxes			
Rent			
Home/Condo/Townhome Dues			
Home/Condo/Townhome Maintenance Fees			
Home Security System			
Miscellaneous			

2. Insurance	Self	Spouse	Business
Homeowner's/Renter's Insurance			
Automobile			
Health			
Dental			
Vision			
Life			
Disability			
Umbrella			
Long-Term Care			
Prescription Plan			
Miscellaneous			

3. Loan Payments	Self	Spouse	Child(ren)	Business
Federal Student Loan(s)				
Private Student Loan(s)				
Education Expense for Child				
Education Expense for Grandchild				
Vehicle 1 Payment/Lease				
Vehicle 2 Payment/Lease				
Personal Loan				
Business Loan				
Miscellaneous				

TOTAL				

Monthly Variable Expenses (next 4 pages)

1. Savings

	Self	Spouse
Emergency savings		
Sinking fund to replace cars (if applicable)		
Sinking fund for major home repairs		

2. Retirement Savings

IRA contributions		
Roth IRA contributions		
401(k) contributions		
Defined benefit contributions		
Pension contributions		
SEP contributions		
HSA contributions		

3. Travel

Vacations		
Local weekend trips		
Domestic flight expenses		
International flight expenses		
Fees		

4. Children/Education

Books		
Supplies		
Computer/electronics		
529 Plan gifting/contributions		
Daycare expenses		

5. Cash Gifts

Charitable donations	
Holiday gifts	
Graduation gifts	
Birthday gifts	
Annual gifts to children, grandchildren	

	1st Home	2nd Home

6. Utilities
Electricity
Gas
Water

7. Communication Services
Cable/Satellite Television
Internet
Home Telephone
Cellular Telephone
Computers/Laptops
Other Service

	Self	Spouse

8. Food and Beverages
Groceries
Fast Food and Convenience
Wine/Liquor/Alcohol

9. Transportation
Fuel
Vehicle Maintenance / Oil Changes
Toll Fees
Public Transportation Fares
Parking
Miscellaneous

10. Household
Cleaning Services
Landscaping Services
Household Repairs/Services
Furnishings and Appliances
Kitchen Items and Supplies
Laundry Supplies
Snow Removal
Pool Cleaning and Maintenance
Miscellaneous

11. Pets

	Self	Spouse
Food		
Veterinary		
Dogwalking Services		
Grooming		
Boarding Services		
Pet Sitting		

12. Personal

Hair Styling (cuts, colors, etc.)		
Personal Health and Beauty Items		
Dry Cleaning		
Gym Membership		

13. Medical and Pharmacy

Prescriptions and OTC Medicine		
Medical Coinsurance and Deductibles		
Eyeglasses/Contact Lenses		
Dental/Orthodontic Work		
Other Unreimbursed Medical Expenses		

14. Personal Attire

Clothing		
Footwear		
Accessories		
Miscellaneous Items		
Jewelry		

15. Entertainment and Dining	Self	Spouse
Movie, Theatre, Concert Tickets		
Newspaper and Magazine Subscriptions		
Internet Media/Subscriptions		
Hobby Equipment, Supplies, and Material		
Golf Club Memberships and Dues		
Classes/Lessons (Recreational) for Self		
Dining Out		
Dinner Parties		
Miscellaneous		

16. Miscellaneous		
Professional Fees (CPA, attorney, etc.)		

17. Family Support		
Support for Elderly Parents		
Support for Children		
Support for Grandchildren		

TOTAL		

TOTAL INCOME (page 1) $_____
LESS FIXED EXPENSES (page 2)   ($_____)
LESS VARIABLE EXPENSES (pages 3–5)   ($_____)
NET CASH FLOW $_____

Social Security Administration

Checklist For Online Medicare, Retirement, and Spouses Applications

This checklist will help you gather the information you may need to complete the online Medicare, Retirement, and Spouse's applications. We recommend you print this page to use while you gather your information. We hope you find our online application easy and convenient.

Information	Medicare Only	Retirement and/or Spouses
Date and Place of Birth If you were born outside the United States or its territories: • Name of your birth country at the time of your birth (it may have a different name now) • Permanent Resident Card number (if you are not a U.S citizen)	X	X
Medicaid (state health insurance) Number & Start and End Dates	X	
Current Health Insurance • Employment start and end dates for the current employer (of you or your spouse) who provides your health insurance coverage through a Group Health Plan • Start and end dates for the Group Health Insurance provided by you (or your spouse's) current employer	X	
Marriage and Divorce • Name of current spouse • Name of prior spouse (if the marriage lasted more than 10 years or ended in death) • Spouse(s) date of birth and SSN (optional) • Beginning and ending dates of marriage(s) • Place of marriage(s) (city, state or country, if married outside the U.S.)		X
Names and Dates of Birth of Children Who • Became disabled prior to age 22, or • Are under age 18 and are unmarried, or • Are aged 18 to 19 and still attending secondary school full time		X
U.S. Military Service • Type of duty and branch • Service period dates		X
Employer Details for Current Year and Prior 2 Years (not self-employment) • View your Social Security Statement online at http://www.socialsecurity.gov/myaccount/ • Employer name • Employment start and end dates		X
Self-Employment Details for Current Year and Prior 2 Years • View your Social Security Statement online at http://www.socialsecurity.gov/myaccount/ • Business type • Total net income		X

Direct Deposit:
 Domestic bank (USA)   **International bank (non-USA)**
 • Account type and number   • International Direct Deposit (IDD) bank country
 • Bank routing number   • Bank name, bank code, and currency
      • Account type and number
      • Branch/transit number
		X

We may contact you for additional information after you submit your online application.

Medicare Costs at a Glance

2014 Costs at a Glance	
2014 Part B premium	Most people pay $104.90 each month.
Part B deductible	$147 per year
Part A premium	Most people don't pay a monthly premium for Part A. If you buy Part A, you'll pay up to $426 each month.
Part A hospital inpatient deductible	You pay: · $1,216 deductible for each benefit period · Days 1–60: $0 coinsurance for each benefit period · Days 61–90: $304 coinsurance per day of each benefit period · Days 91 and beyond: $608 coinsurance per each "lifetime reserve day" after day 90 for each benefit period (up to 60 days over your lifetime) · Beyond lifetime reserve days: all costs

Medicare Costs at a Glance

Medicare Part B (Medical Insurance)

Most people pay the Part B premium of $104.90 each month.

However, if your modified adjusted gross income as reported on your IRS tax return from two years ago is above a certain amount, you may pay more.

If your yearly income in 2012 (for what you pay in 2014) was			You pay (in 2014)
File individual tax return	**File joint tax return**	**File married and separate tax return**	
$85,000 or less	$170,000 or less	$85,000 or less	$104.90
above $85,000 up to $107,000	above $170,000 up to $214,000	not applicable	$146.90
above $107,000 up to $160,000	above $214,000 up to $320,000	not applicable	$209.80
above $160,000 up to $214,000	above $320,000 up to $428,000	above $85,000 and up to $129,000	$272.70
above $214,000	above $428,000	above $129,000	$335.70

Medicare Costs at a Glance

Medicare Part D (Medicare prescription drug coverage)

The Part D monthly premium varies by plan (higher-income consumers may pay more).

The chart below shows your estimated prescription drug plan monthly premium based on your income as reported on your IRS tax return from two years ago. If your income is above a certain limit, you'll pay an income-related monthly adjustment amount in addition to your plan premium.

If your filing status and yearly income in 2012 was			
File individual tax return	**File joint tax return**	**File married and separate tax return**	**You pay (in 2014)**
$85,000 or less	$170,000 or less	$85,000 or less	your plan premium
above $85,000 up to $107,000	above $170,000 up to $214,000	not applicable	$12.10 + your plan premium
above $107,000 up to $160,000	above $214,000 up to $320,000	not applicable	$31.10 + your plan premium
above $160,000 up to $214,000	above $320,000 up to $428,000	above $85,000 up to $129,000	$50.20 + your plan premium
above $214,000	above $428,000	above $129,000	$69.30 + your plan

www.medicare.gov/your-medicare-costs/costs-at-a-glance/

Vast resources on the topic of retirement are readily available on the internet. Still, like every journey of discovery it often helps to have a starting point. To that end I've listed some particularly useful sources of information found during the process of writing this book. These resources and others are also listed on the associated website, but having this list might be useful as a starting point.

Social Security

▶ **How to Apply for Retirement Benefits**
http://www.socialsecurity.gov/planners/about.htm

▶ **All About Medicare**
http://www.medicare.gov/

▶ **Calculator to Determine Your Full Retirement Age**
http://www.ssa.gov/pubs/ageincrease.htm

▶ **Quickly Estimate Your Retirement Benefits** https://secure.ssa.gov/acu/ACU_KBA/main.jsp?URL=/apps8z/ARPI/main.jsp?locale=en&LVL=4

Retirement

▶ **Get an Accurate Estimate of Your Retirement Benefits**
   http://www.socialsecurity.gov/OACT/anypia/anypia.html

▶ **Estimate the Future Worth of Your Social Security Benefits**
   http://www.socialsecurity.gov/OACT/quickcalc/index.html

▶ **Get an Estimate of How Long You'll Live**
   (http://www.socialsecurity.gov/oact/population/longevity.html)

▶ **Life Expectancy Statistics**
   http://life-span.findthebest.com/d/d/90

Financial and Legal Exploration

▶ **Basic Financial and Investing Terminology Resource**
   http://www.investopedia.com/

▶ **Investor Educational Resource List**
   http://www.sec.gov/investor/links.shtml

▶ **Most Comprehensive Free Financial Website**
   http://www.bankrate.com/

▶ **How Inflation Impacts Saving Accounts**
   http://apps.finra.org/Calcs/1/Savings

▶ **All About the Impact of Inflation**
   http://inflationdata.com/

▶ **Reliable Retirement Resource**
http://www.aarp.org/

▶ **Accessible Investment and Financial Information**
http://www.nerdwallet.com/

▶ **Useful Financial Tools and Calculators**
http://www.finra.org/Investors/ToolsCalculators/

▶ **Helpful Financial Advice and Information**
https://www.mint.com/blog/

▶ **Money and Investing Resource for Everyone**
http://www.fool.com

▶ **Useful Legal Term Resource and Dictionary**
http://www.thefreedictionary.com/
http://www.nolo.com/

▶ **All About Gifting**
http://www.pgdc.com/

REFERENCES

Chapter 1

1. Social Security Administration, "Life Expectancy for Social Security," http://www.ssa.gov/history/lifeexpect.html.
2. Social Security Administration, "Calculators: Life Expectancy," http://www.ssa.gov/planners/life-expectancy.htm.
3. Walter Updegrave, "Do I Really Need My Savings to Last Until I'm 100?" CNN Money, April 27, 2012, http://money.cnn.com/2012/04/27/pf/expert/life-expectancy-retirement.moneymag/.
4. Employee Benefit Research Institute, "History of Pension Plans," http://www.ebri.org/publications/facts/index.cfm?fa=0398afact.
5. Tom Anderson, "Your 401(k): When It Was Invented—and Why," LearnVest, http://www.learnvest.com/knowledge-center/your-401k-when-it-was-invented-and-why/.

Chapter 2

1. Annamaria Lusardi and Olivia S. Mitchell, "Debt and Debt Management among Older Adults," 15th Annual Joint Meeting of the Retirement Research Consortium, August 1–2, 2013, Washington, DC, http://www.mrrc.isr.umich.edu/transmit/rrc2013/summaries/4A_LusardiMitchellSummary.pdf.
2. Ibid.
3. "Casey Jones," words by Robert Hunter, music by Jerry Garcia (1970).
4. Inside Mortgage Finance, http://www.insidemortgagefinance.com/
5. NerdWallet, "American Household Credit Card Statistics: 2014," http://www.nerdwallet.com/blog/credit-card-data/average-credit-card-debt-household/.
6. Cost of a Wedding, http://www.costofwedding.com/.
7. Jordan Weissmann, "Here's Exactly How Many College Graduates Live Back at Home," *The Atlantic*, February 26, 2013, http://www.theatlantic.com/business/archive/2013/02/heres-exactly-how-many-college-graduates-live-back-at-home/273529/.

8. Melanie Hicken, "Average Cost to Raise a Kid: $241,080," CNN Money, August 14, 2013, http://money.cnn.com/2013/08/14/pf/cost-children/.

9. Glenn Curtis, "Reverse Mortgage Pitfalls," Investopedia, May 20, 2010, http://www.investopedia.com/articles/mortgages-real-estate/08/reverse-mortgage.asp

10. Paul Taylor, Kim Parker, Eileen Patten, Seth Motel, "The Sandwich Generation: Rising Financial Burdens for Middle-Aged Americans," PewResearchCenter Social & Demographic Trends, January 30, 2013, http://www.pewsocialtrends.org/files/2013/01/Sandwich_Generation_Report_FI-NAL_1-29.pdf.

11. U.S. Department of Health and Human Services, "Costs of Care," http://longtermcare.gov/costs-how-to-pay/costs-of-care/.

12. The Henry J. Kaiser Family Foundation, "2013 Employer Health Benefits Survey," August 20, 2013, http://kff.org/private-insurance/report/2013-employer-health-benefits/.

13. Michael Lawrence Frank, "Limited Medical Benefits Plans: What Insurance Conpanies, Employers and Reinsurers Need to Know," *Reinsurance Section Newsletter*, August 2008, http://www.soa.org/search.aspx?go=True&q=private+insurance+costs+for+health+care&page=1&page-size=10&or=True.

Chapter 3

1. US Inflation Calculator, "Historical Inflation Rates 1914–2014," http://www.usinflationcalculator.com/inflation/historical-inflation-rates/.

2. US Census, "Median and Average Sales Prices of New Homes Sold in United States," http://www.census.gov/const/uspriceann.pdf.

3. National Center for Education Statistics, Digest of Educational Statistics, "Table 320. Average Undergraduate Tuition and Fees and Room and Board Rates Charged for Full-Time Students in Degree-Granting Institutions, by Type and Control of Institution: 1964–65 through 2006–07," http://nces.ed.gov/programs/digest/d07/tables/dt07_320.asp.

4. Sheyna Steiner, "Is Inflation Higher than You Think?" Bankrate.com, http://www.bankrate.com/finance/personal-finance/is-inflation-higher-than-you-think-1.aspx.

5. Ashley Henshaw, "What Is the Average Cost of Homeowners Insurance," http://homeguides.sfgate.com/average-cost-homeowners-insurance-3020.html/

6. MetLife, "Market Survey of Long-Term Care Costs," https://www.metlife.com/mmi/research/2012-market-survey-long-term-care-costs.html#keyfindings.

Chapter 4

1. Bloomberg Businessweek Magazine, "Nightmare Mortgages," September 10, 2006, http://www.businessweek.com/stories/2006-09-10/nightmare-mortgages.

2. Investorpedia, "Definition of 'Bond,'" http://www.investopedia.com/terms/b/bond.asp.

3. Wikipedia, "Black Monday (1987)," http://en.wikipedia.org/wiki/Black_Monday_(1987).

4. Wikipedia, "The Bubble Bursts," http://en.wikipedia.org/wiki/Dot-com_bubble#The_bubble_bursts.

5. Kimberly Amadeo, "Stock Market History," About.com, http://useconomy.about.com/od/stock-marketcomponents/a/Dow_History.htm.

6. Jane McGrath, "Did the Dutch Really Trade Manhattan for Nutmeg?" How Stuff Works, http://history.howstuffworks.com/history-vs-myth/nutmeg-new-netherland1.htm.

7. Easycalculation.com, "Compound Interest Calculator," http://easycalculation.com/compound-interest.php.

8. Wikipedia, "1998 Russian Financial Crisis," http://en.wikipedia.org/wiki/1998_Russian_financial_crisis.

9. Bankrate.com, "National CD Rates for March 27, 2014," http://www.bankrate.com/finance/cd/rate-roundup.aspx.

10. Forcastchart.com, "Six Month CD Interest Rate Forecast," http://forecast-chart.com/year-cd-interest.html.

11. Investorpedia, "Sequence Risk," http://www.investopedia.com/terms/s/sequence-risk.asp.

12. U.S. Security and Exchange Commission, "Annuities," http://www.sec.gov/answers/annuity.htm.

Chapter 5

1. Social Security Administration, "The 2012 Annual Report of the Board of Trustees of the Federal Old-Age and Survivors Insurance and Federal Disability Insurance Trust Funds," April 25, 2012, http://www.ssa.gov/OACT/TR/2012/tr2012.pdf.

2. Pew Research Center, "Baby Boomers Retire," December 29, 2010, http://www.pewresearch.org/daily-number/baby-boomers-retire/.

3. Social Security Administration, "When Did Social Security Start?" https://faq.ssa.gov/ics/support/KBAnswer.asp?questionID=1849&hitOffset=15+14+13+11&docID=6877

4. Social Security Administration: http://www.socialsecurity.gov/cola/2014/factsheet.htmA.

5. Social Security Administration, "History of Automatic Cost-of-Living Adjustments," http://www.ssa.gov/cola/automatic-cola.htm.

6. Social Security Administration, "Retirement Planner: Full Retirement Age," http://www.ssa.gov/retire2/retirechart.htm.

7. D'Vera Cohn, Jeffrey S. Passel, Wendy Wang, and Gretchen Livingston, "Barely Half of U.S. Adults Are Married: A Record Low," Pew Research Center, http://www.pewsocialtrends.org/2011/12/14/barely-half-of-u-s-adults-are-married-a-record-low/.

8. Social Security Administration, "How Much Can I Earn While Receiving Social Security Retirement Benefits?" https://faq.ssa.gov/ics/support/kbanswer.asp?deptID=34019&questionID=1933&task=knowledge.

Chapter 6

1. Christina LaMontagne, "NerdWallet Health Finds Medical Bankruptcy Accounts for Majority of Personal Bankruptcies, NerdWallet, March 26, 2014, http://www.nerdwallet.com/blog/health/2014/03/26/medical-bankruptcy/.

2. Wikipedia, "History of Healthcare Reform in the United States," http://en.wikipedia.org/wiki/History_of_health_care_reform_in_the_United_States.

3. The Henry J. Kaiser Family Foundation, "2013 Employer Health Benefits Survey," Kaiser Family Foundation, August 20, 2013, http://kff.org/private-insurance/report/2013-employer-health-benefits/.

4. Caroline Humer, "Obamacare's Average Monthly Cost Across US: $328," MSN News, September 9, 2013, http://news.msn.com/us/obamacares-average-monthly-cost-across-us-dollar328?stay=1.

5. HeathCare.gov, "How Does the Healthcare Law Protect Me," https://www.healthcare.gov/how-does-the-health-care-law-protect-me/.

6. Physicians for a National Health Program, "A Brief History: Universal Healthcare Efforts in the US," http://www.pnhp.org/facts/a-brief-history-universal-health-care-efforts-in-the-us.

7. Department of Health & Human Services, "What's Medicare," August 2013, http://www.medicare.gov/Pubs/pdf/11306.pdf.

8. Medicare.gov, "Medicaid," http://www.medicare.gov/your-medicare-costs/help-paying-costs/medicaid/medicaid.html.

9. Iain M. Carey, Sunil M. Shah, Stephen DeWilde, Tess Harris, Christina R. Victor, and Derek G. Cook, "Increased Risk of Acute Cardiovascular Events After Partner Bereavement," JAMA Internal Medicine, 2014.

10. MetLife, "Market Survey of Long-Term Care Costs, https://www.metlife.com/mmi/research/2012-market-survey-long-term-care-costs.html#keyfindings.

11. BBC Research, "Disabled and Elderly Assistive Technologies," http://www.bccresearch.com/market-research/healthcare/disabled-elderly-assist-technologies-hlc047d.html.

Chapter 7

1. American Institute of CPAs, "Estate and Trust Impact of 3.8% Net Investment Income Tax," http://www.aicpa.org/interestareas/tax/resources/trustestateandgift/toolsandaids/pages/estateandtrustimpactof38medicaresurtax.aspx.

Chapter 8

1. Jeanine Skowronski, "A Matter of Trust: Naming a Trustee Is a Key Estate-Planning Decision. And One of the Toughest," Wall Street Journal, September 10, 2012, http://online.wsj.com/news/articles/SB10000872396390444025204577544900770188834.

2. G. M. Filisko, "Choose the Right Executor or Trustee: 5 Tips for a Decision that Can Make or Break Estate Planning," AARP, April 22, 2011, http://www.aarp.org/money/estate-planning/info-04-2011/choosing-right-executor-trustee.html.

3. N. Brian Caverly and Jordan S. Simon, "Revocable versus Irrevocable Trusts," For Dummies, http://www.dummies.com/how-to/content/revocable-versus-irrevocable-trusts.html.

4. NOLO, "Estate and Gift Tax FAQ," http://www.nolo.com/legal-encyclopedia/estate-gift-tax-faq-29136.html.

5. AICPA, 529 Plans and Estate Planning, http://www.aicpa.org/interestareas/personalfinancialplan-

ning/resources/practicecenter/forefieldadvisor/downloadabledocuments/ff529plansandestateplan-ningpresentation.pdf.

6. National Philanthropic Trust, "Charitable Giving Statistics," http://www.nptrust.org/philanthrop-ic-resources/charitable-giving-statistics.

Chapter 9

1. Bowling Green State University, "Marriage Rate Lowest in a Century," http://www2.bgsu.edu/offices/mc/news/2013/news133952.html.

2. Mark Banschick, "The High Failure Rate of Second and Third Marriages," Psychology Today, February 6, 2012, http://www.psychologytoday.com/blog/the-intelligent-divorce/201202/the-high-failure-rate-second-and-third-marriages.

3. Centers for Disease Control and Prevention, "National Marriage and Divorce Rate Trends," http://www.cdc.gov/nchs/nvss/marriage_divorce_tables.htm.

4. Cragman.com, "How Old Is the Average Widow or Widower?" http://www.cragman.com/age.htm.

5. Social Security Administration, "Income of the Population 55 or Older, 2008," April 2010, http://www.ssa.gov/policy/docs/statcomps/income_pop55/2008/incpop08.pdf.